property

www.thegoodwebguide.co.uk

thegoodwebguide

property:
the essential guide to buying, selling and renting property online

Mike Miller

The Good Web Guide Limited • London

First Published in Great Britain in 2003 by The Good Web Guide Limited
65 Bromfelde Road, London SW4 6PP

www.thegoodwebguide.co.uk

Email:feedback@thegoodwebguide.co.uk

© 2003 The Good Web Guide Ltd

Text © 2003 Mike Miller

Original series concept by Steve Bailey.

10 9 8 7 6 5 4 3 2 1

A catalogue record for this book is available from the British Library.

ISBN 1-903282-44-6

The publishers and author have done their best to ensure the accuracy and currency of all information in this volume, however they can accept no responsibility for any loss or inconvenience sustained by any reader as a result of its information or advice.

All rights reserved. No part of this publication may be reproduced, transmitted or stored in a retrieval system, in any form or by any means, except for the quotation of brief passages in reviews without permission in writing from The Good Web Guide Ltd.

Design by Myriad Creative Ltd

Printed in Italy at LEGO S.p.A.

contents

the good web guides	6
introduction	8
user key	10
1 review of the property market	11
2 finding the right property	17
3 check out the local area	69
4 selecting the right mortgage	76
5 need help to move?	97
6 all about the house	103
7 protect your assets	107
professional and trade organisations	112
glossary for the property market	114
index	129

the good web guides

The World Wide Web is a vast resource, with millions of sites on every conceivable subject. There are people who have made it their mission to surf the net: cyber-communities have grown, and people have formed relationships and even married on the net.

However, the reality for most people is that they don't have the time or inclination to surf the net for hours on end. Busy people want to use the internet for quick access to information. You don't have to spend hours on the internet looking for answers to your questions and you don't have to be an accomplished net surfer or cyber wizard to get the most out of the web. It can be a quick and useful resource if you are looking for specific information.

The Good Web Guides have been published with this in mind. To give you a head start in your search, our researchers have looked at hundreds of sites and what you will find in the Good Web Guides is a collection of reviews of the best we've found.

The Good Web Guide recommendation is impartial and all the sites have been visited several times. Reviews are focused on the website and what it sets out to do, rather than an endorsement of a company, or their product. A small but beautiful site run by a one-man band may be rated higher than an ambitious but flawed site run by a mighty organisation.

Relevance to the UK-based visitor is also given a high premium: tantalising as it is to read about purchases you can make in California, because of delivery charges, import duties and controls it may not be as useful as a local site.

Our reviewers considered a number of questions when reviewing the sites, such as: How quickly do the sites and individual pages download? Can you move around the site easily and get back to where you started, and do the links work? Is the information up to date and accurate? And is the site pleasing to the eye and easy to read? More importantly, we also asked whether the site has something distinctive to offer, whether it be entertainment, inspiration or pure information. On the basis of the answers to these questions sites are given ratings out of five. As we aim only to include sites that we feel are of serious interest, there are very few low-rated sites.

Bear in mind that the collection of reviews you see here are just a snapshot of the sites at a particular time. The process of choosing and writing about sites is rather like painting the Forth Bridge: as each section appears complete, new sites are launched and others are modified. When you've registered at the Good Web Guide site you can check out the reviews of new sites and updates of existing ones, or even have them emailed to you.

By registering at **www.thegoodwebguide.co.uk** you'll find hot links to all the sites listed, so you can just click and go without needing to type the addresses accurately into your browser.

As this is the first edition of the Good Web Guide Property, all our sites have been reviewed by the author and research team, but we'd like to know what you think. Contact us via the website or email feedback@thegoodwebguide.co.uk. You are welcome to recommend sites, quibble about the ratings, point out changes and inaccuracies or suggest new features to assess.

You can find us at **www.thegoodwebguide.co.uk**

introduction

There is no doubt that along with pensions the purchase of a house is the largest and most important investment people ever make. And to improve matters, there has always been a remarkably generous regime surrounding the tax treatment of houses. There is no capital gains tax on the sale of a main residence. This offers special advantages when you retire and may wish to trade down, or even move abroad.

The surprising thing is that most people pay more attention to ascertaining the condition of a second hand car than they do finding out about their new family home. This could be said to reflect as much on the archaic system for house purchase in the UK rather than the purchasers themselves.

The revolution in technology brought mixed blessings. For some the lure of success was dashed as investors realised the internet did not produce the productivity gains they had hoped for.

But in some areas the reverse is true. Property is one such area.

For a long time property sales had an image of an independent, dispersed industry with little central organization. But not any more. The industry has been turned from a local service for local people by local people into a national industry with close links to the financial services sector.

The internet is consolidating this change. Even the smallest estate agency now realizes that it has to change to survive.

The aim of getting more prospective purchasers to view property remains exactly the same. The industry has realised that many prospective buyers have access to computers both at home and at work. And as a marketing tool for residential property the internet offers opportunities never before available to the industry.

The remarkable thing about this revolution in the property market is that it is so obviously to everyone's advantage.

For the estate agent, viewings are frequently more purposeful, and conversion rates are increased. And the consumer saves time and reduces inconvenience. Consumers are able to view a much larger section of the market from the comfort of their own home.

The internet enhances the work estate agents do. But it does not replace them. The new technology offers better selection, but it can't take the decision to buy. A visit to a new property remains essential. Thus a substantial section of the public now view the internet as the starting point for property searches. It is quite simply the best way to compile a short list of properties to view.

But the success of the internet has become a problem in itself. There is now so much information available that confusion reigns. Reference books are thus needed to guide the searcher to the better websites, and to give them the additional time that is so readily acknowledged as one of the major advantages of the net.

On the internet the property market is incestuous. Everyone is trying to sell everything, including one another's properties! The property net is a jungle. The websites understand that agents will not necessarily commit exclusively to one site.

But we have selected those sites that will successfully take you through the whole process from your first thought of moving to closing your new front door.

Moving house is stressful, and the legwork involved is a factor adding to that stress. But if the legwork is reduced – so is stress. And that is good news in anyone's book!

user key

£	subscription required
R	registration required
🔒	secure online ordering
UK	United Kingdom
US	United States

Chapter 01

review of the property market

While the importance of the financial decision on house purchase is fully acknowledged, it is surprising that we don't always fully investigate the basis of those decisions.

The type of property we buy is largely determined by family circumstances, financial resources, employment and general economic conditions. But do we always give full consideration to the geographical variations in the property market, and the timing of a possible move?

It is clear that there are significant regional variations within the United Kingdom. Even a cursory glance at the figures would show that regions do not grow at the same rate year-on-year.

For the commuter in particular, the geographical options open to him around our major conurbations are significant. Careful choice of location could add thousands of pounds to his total wealth over a relatively short period of time.

Not everyone is able to select the precise time of a move. There may be no choice. But when circumstances are such that choice is possible, it makes sense to base decisions of timing and geography on accepted market facts.

This sort of approach is not attempting to play the market but is an attempt to look at market circumstances from a historical point of view and to make sensible decisions as to whether to proceed or not. And if so, which areas offer the best opportunity.

No one information site gives the complete answer. But it is possible to gain significant market insight, and to see what the most experienced practitioners in the industry, and the most prestigious organisations, are saying. And considering the average financial outlay, it would be madness not to use the information and views available. At the worst you sensibly protect your significant investment. At best, you maximise your gain by understanding the market.

Main Information Sites

To find out what is really happening in the property market, have a look at our recommendations below.

www.nationwide.co.uk			
Nationwide			
Overall rating: ★ ★ ★ ★			
Classification: Building Society		**Readability:**	★ ★ ★ ★
Updating: Monthly		**Content:**	★ ★ ★ ★
Navigation: ★ ★ ★ ★		**Speed:**	★ ★ ★ ★
UK			

Nationwide offers a very comprehensive website with a good section on housing statistics.

The area we wish to examine is within the Site contents. This is to be found at the top right-hand side of the homepage. This presents a drop down menu. Click on House Prices Index. Alternatively you can go in via Site Tools – Your House Price. This is on the left hand side of the homepage.

This immediately brings up the Nationwide House Prices Site. This site deals with a full range of matters relating to house prices.

The Monthly and Quarterly review are recognised as one of the leading authorities on house price movements and forecasts. It presents a review of the previous months figures and then computes new quarterly and annual figures in the light of these new figures.

More importantly, there follows the latest economic predictions for the immediate period ahead, and the following year.

The Historical Data will allow you to view previously published monthly and quarterly press releases. You can download and view house price data of your own choice. The monthly and quarterly reviews are simple drop down menus from which you merely select the appropriate date.

The house price data is presented in 12 different variations of property. Each one is offered with an appropriate time scale in relation to the statistics. Examples are Flats (post 1991) and Older Properties (post 1973).

SPECIAL FEATURES

The Nationwide Price Index shows Real Price against Real Trend from the 1950s. Knowledge of this graph is essential if a prospective purchaser is to make judgements on the property cycle.

The Calculator allows you to calculate a price for your property. Only a few basic parameters are required. This includes a valuation with a year. This could be at the time of purchase, or some subsequent valuation. A date to which you wish the new valuation to be taken must be entered. The calculator will also help you in deciding your correct area for entry into the calculation.

This site is a must. It will make decisions on property that much more professional. The material is excellent.

www.hbosplc.com
Halifax

Overall rating: ★ ★ ★ ★			
Classification:	Building Society	**Readability:**	★ ★ ★
Updating:	Monthly	**Content:**	★ ★ ★ ★
Navigation:	★ ★ ★ ★	**Speed:**	★ ★ ★ ★

UK

Halifax takes the largest share of the mortgage market in the United Kingdom. Not surprisingly, their view of what is happening and what is likely to happen in the market place is of paramount importance.

The Halifax House Price Index has been an institution since inception in 1984. The index is used by government departments, media and business as an authoritative indication of house price movements in the UK. It is based on the largest sample of housing data and provides the longest unbroken series of any similar UK index.

From the homepage the left hand tool bar has a button showing Economic View. This section contains an assessment of the economy, including trends in the UK, and the Halifax House Price Index.

Also within this section is the Economic Outlook, providing a five-year view on the prospects for global and UK economies.

National Commentary and Analysis provides the immediate coverage of the previous month and the new forecast for the remainder of the year. It also updates the new annual forecast.

The site also contains a comprehensive table of House Price Indices that include percentage change, standard average price, and more importantly national average earnings and price/earnings ratios. These are key figures in understanding the possible movement of future prices. There is also important data on First Time Buyers and Former Owner Occupiers (All Houses).

SPECIAL FEATURES

The Latest Regional Summary is excellent. By placing your pointer onto the desired area of the United Kingdom you obtain current house price statistics. It is possible to print out the whole Regional Quarterly Summary if desired. Quarterly Regional Comments are available for some 12 regions throughout the UK if required.

The House Price Calculator indicates how average prices within each UK region have moved over the last few years. Details required are the region, the house price at the start of the computation, and the dates for the computation. The results indicate how the house has risen in value.

The Historical Data Spreadsheet downloads all the Halifax indices back to 1983.

Two final sections include an article on the Methodology applied, and a Timetable giving publication dates of the monthly reports.

This site is for everyone who takes house purchasing seriously. It is not to be missed.

www.thegoodwebguide.co.uk **13**

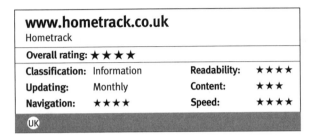

www.hometrack.co.uk
Hometrack

Overall rating: ★★★★			
Classification:	Information	**Readability:**	★★★★
Updating:	Monthly	**Content:**	★★★
Navigation:	★★★★	**Speed:**	★★★★

UK

The Hometrack index is designed to give up-to-date and accurate information about prices and trends down to postcode level. The service was launched in September 2000. Information is gathered from nearly 5,000 estate agents. Comparisons are based on transactions agreed in the previous month.

The Homepage gives immediate access to the Latest News and Prices and Trends facility.

Latest News gives details of last month's performance by region, as well as other information. All that is required for Prices and Trends is to enter the postcode of the area you wish to enquire about. The search results come in the form of a Price Update. This is a series of easy-to-read graphs.

The first set relates to the average house prices and trends in the area under investigation. The second set relates to the three-month price trends for a larger area containing the postcode.

The first bar chart in both sets shows property prices across four types of property. These are terraced, semi-detached, detached and flats or maisonettes. The second chart indicates price trends across these four categories over the past four months. A third chart shows the average price of these four categories over a three-month period and the percentage price change.

SPECIAL FEATURES

Market Activity This is an expression of the pace of activity on the market. It shows the Time to Sell (in weeks) and the number of Viewings per Sale. Also given with these figures is the time taken to get an agreed sale. As with the Price Update, these figures are repeated for a wider area.

Market Demand This shows how many Registered Buyers there are with the estate agent in a given month. A change in the number of buyers is a good indication of future demand. Additionally the graph shows the position on the number of New Instructions. This shows whether the number has increased or decreased.

Change in Sales This shows either an increase or decrease in the number of offers that have been accepted by sellers. This figure gives a good indication of market strength.

A final chart shows in simple percentage terms the numbers of buyers registered, the instructions on the books and the changes in sales over the past three months.

These graphs and figures are very simple yet very powerful. You cannot fail to improve your knowledge of the housing market with a visit to this site.

Other Useful Information Sites

The Wriglesworth Consultancy
www.wriglesworth.com

The site includes current research papers on the property market, topical comments and opinions, and regular articles on property written for the *Mail on Sunday*.

This is an excellent site to update your knowledge of the property market. It is clear and easy to read.

BBC
www.bbc.co.uk/rightmoves

There is a mass of common-sense information on this site. It includes a UK price guide, the latest property news and expert advice on a range of property issues.

This is a useful site for the homeowner who wants the main issues set out in a simple and readable fashion.

Property Prices
www.proviser.com

The site contains some useful charts on house prices. With the price-trend graphs there is the ability to see how prices have changed over time. Price can be compared using town and postcode. The figures come from HM Land Registry.

Council of Mortgage Lenders
www.cml.org.uk

The CML is the trade association for mortgage lenders in the UK. Its members undertake around 98% of UK residential mortgages. The Press Releases site has a range of articles as well as mortgage lending figures for the previous month.

This site represents the latest information available on the property market. It is a must for anyone who wishes to update themselves on current market conditions. It also offers some views on the future.

HM Land Registry
www.landreg.gov.uk

The website does not offer access to live data. But it does offer a property price database where you can find average prices of residential property in England and Wales. It is a detailed and authoritative insight into what is actually happening to average prices and sales volumes in the residential property market.

The HM Land Registry Residential Property Price Report is issued quarterly. The report is intended to complement information available from other sources. But the advantage of this report is that it is free from hype. It tells you what really happened.

Your Mortgage
www.yourmortgage.co.uk

The Property Prices menu on the Homepage will produce a price prediction for your property over the next five years. Simply enter the postcode and type of property. If the property was bought after 1996 it is possible to enter additional information to obtain a more accurate prediction. This is a quick and useful calculator.

British Bankers Association
www.bba.org.uk

Click on Statistics, and then on Statistical Releases for Major British Banking Groups and you will display the monthly statements on Mortgage Lending and Lending to Individuals. This gives a good indication of the way the market is moving.

Chapter 02

finding the right property

The majority of people who are looking to move home in the next 12 months will use the internet to search for property, and it offers virtually everything for those interested in property – no matter what sort of property and what sort of related activity.

Properties are on display 24 hours per day, 365 days a year. There are now over 100 sites.

Rapid improvements in site development are tangible signs that as a marketing tool this medium is succeeding. Estate agents have realised that it makes sense to replace a limited shop window display with an almost limitless display.

Potential customers can view properties in their own time and in their own home. And the displays are more informative, imaginative and interactive.

What appears to be clear is that users prefer to search the larger sites. A number of local estate agents will be present on the site, allowing movement to the local site itself for further information or enquiries.

There is an obvious divide between corporate sites and private sites. Private sites are not as good, and there are problems ahead for the private purchaser.

If we thought estate agents were bad at describing property, we now have someone who is worse – the private seller!

Estate agents are bound by the Property Misdescriptions Act, which outlaws embellishment. But private sellers do not have to comply with this law and can describe their property as they see fit. And current experience suggests that more often than not they give full vent to their imagination!

Additionally with private sales there is a major problem with pricing. There is always the danger that the seller will attempt to push up the price.

Two other problems concern the timing of visits and security. Estate agents are clearly more flexible with timing. Viewings should never be undertaken alone.

Property Directories

The directories listed below function like an address book or a telephone directory. They link you to any site listed. But in the following pages we review the best property sites available for you. These include conventional as well as specialist property websites.

UK Property Guide
www.ukpropertyguide.co.uk

The site covers buying, selling and renting properties in the UK. Also included is a Direct Sales section that allows you to cut out the middleman and to buy and sell your property direct.

Over 70 property sites are listed, all with a grading. All the property listings are linked directly to their own sites so searching is quick. This is a good directory site for showing you what is available. And it allows you to get around them at a reasonable speed.

The Move Channel
www.themovechannel.com

This is a site that offers much more than just a directory list of property sites for buying and selling. The site-finder includes buying, selling, renting and letting, as well as finance and home services. And there is much more on the site – perhaps too much. There are over 160 records on the property database. Navigation is sometimes confusing. It is an interesting site, but don't get lost!

Site Rider
www.siterider.co.uk

There are over 60 property sites listed, but information about each one is not very comprehensive. And there is no assessment of site quality. The site can be searched by region and category.

With 60 sites it must always be worth a visit as the web is changing so quickly.

Housing Net
www.housingnet.co.uk

This is a comprehensive site dealing with many property issues. There is a substantial list of about 70 property web sites. It is currently being refurbished so keep checking.

www.assertahome.com
Asserta

Overall rating: ★ ★ ★ ★			
Classification:	Agency Portal	**Readability:**	★ ★ ★ ★
Updating:	Regularly	**Content:**	★ ★ ★ ★
Navigation:	★ ★ ★ ★ ★	**Speed:**	★ ★ ★ ★

UK

Agency portal Asserta Home is a subsidiary of CGNU, the well-known financial services provider. The site deals with all aspects of home buying and selling and claims to have over 200,000 residential properties on its books.

The site is divided into six main sections. The first three include buying, renting and selling. It provides details about the residential area and local businesses and services.

The mortgages section is powered by Charcol that we review in chapter five.

Legal and Surveying in the locality of choice by postcode or place name

Moving In hosts a link to the website I Have Moved (**www.ihavemoved.com**), enabling you to simultaneously notify about 100 service and product providers (like utility and financial services companies) of your new address. It also contains lists of local removal and storage companies and calculators for comparing the charges of utility providers.

Home Improvement offers help to those with designs on their home.

The homepage provides the ability to search for local estate agents.

The property search tools are most impressive. You can perform a Quick Search or a Full Search. A Quick Search proceeds by price and place name. A Full Search also commences with postcode or place name and allows you to home in on a town or city and to search within a specified geographical radius of up to 20 miles. You can then refine your search by specifiying type of property, price range and whether you require the property to be newly built.

Further search refinements include general specifications (balcony, conservatory, garage, off-street parking), exterior features (swimming pool, paddock, garden, waterfront) and interior features (minimum number of reception rooms and bathrooms).

You can display the search results in ascending order of price or by the closeness of the match to the aforementioned specifications, as measured by the number of bullet points scored.

Another impressive feature of the site is the integration of area information with property details. When you click on a chosen residence you get a description of the property displayed together with links to the estate agent (telephone number, email address and website) and local services and information, plus estimates of typical mortgage outgoings.

An impressive site providing a well-rounded service with high-quality links.

www.findaproperty.com
Findaproperty

Overall rating: ★ ★ ★ ★

Classification:	Real Estate	**Readability:**	★ ★ ★ ★
Updating:	Daily	**Content:**	★ ★ ★
Navigation:	★ ★ ★ ★	**Speed:**	★ ★ ★ ★

UK

Find A Property is an independent and self-financing on-line property magazine. The site was established in April 1994. The site is offered nationwide but concentrates on in-depth coverage of London and the Home Counties.

There are over 64,000 properties advertised from over 1,100 agencies. Over 75% of the properties are advertised with one or more photographs. The site has some Virtual Tours.

SPECIAL FEATURES

Select Your Local Edition is an area selection guide. The material is well laid out and can be viewed at speed. The site shows the property price range for the area. It has a wide range of local links. This is very much a London and south-east site.

Area Guide starts with a search pattern laid out alphabetically. This is very clear and surprisingly comprehensive. Local council tax bands are revealed, as are links to local and county councils. There is a good range of easy-to-read local maps if you cannot find what you want in your immediate area.

Search All Editions brings all the searches together. Input is allowed by price range together with any combination of areas that you wish to explore.

Estate Agents brings together a comprehensive list of estate agents that are grouped alphabetically. Their local operating area is given, together with details.

Up or Down? Although this sub-site gives the impression of telling you what your house is worth, in reality it is a list of articles all relating to the property market. The most recent articles are very useful.

Special Editions Within the special edition feature two sites are worth a visit for the house purchaser. But you may need a big mortgage. The sites are Prestige Homes and Waterside.

A must for the purchaser in the south-east. Fast and full of interest, it is very easy to use.

Fish4homes helps consumers find homes anywhere in the UK. They claim to carry over 218,000 properties in the UK on their books. The service also includes a range of mortgage deals, as well as neighbourhood and risk information. The site contains a range of practical advice and ideas.

Five regional newspaper groups have developed the site. The site also provides services for an additional nine subscriber newspaper groups. Between them, these members represent around 80% of the UK's regional press. This represents more than 800 regional newspapers.

SPECIAL FEATURES

Find a home has four sub-sites. These include Homes for Sale, Homes to Rent and New Developments. The fourth site is named Personal Folder to enhance your own management of the site, including return visits.

Homes for Sale The search tools on the site are well balanced. Locations can be specified either by county, town or postcode. Property descriptions cover all the essential rooms in the house. External features can also be covered. Property particulars vary from satisfactory to very good, with links to maps and demographics.

New Developments can be accessed from the menu bar. The site allows location to be entered, along with the builders name if known. Links are available to location maps and the development website.

The Personal Folder allows you to receive E-mails, save advertisements and to create and save searches. Registration is required. It is free.

OTHER FEATURES

Planning to Buy or Sell has three sub-sites covering a Buyers Guide, a Sellers Guide and Estate Agents. This part of the site is of use to the first time buyer. The Buyers Guide section contains a very quick monthly repayment calculator. Additionally there is a useful field that allows you to search for local estate agents. The Sellers Guide is similarly constructed.

Homebuyer Services offers a substantial Mortgage section, a Legal section, an Insurance section and a Moving section.

The Mortgage Area is worth a visit, and you should visit Mortgage Calculator, which allows you to compute borrowing levels. Mortgage Assistant answers questions on the type of mortgage best suited to you.

Home Improvements covers the three areas of Interiors, DIY, and Getting Help.

This is a good site that has much to offer. Potential buyers should definitely include this site as one to visit.

www.goingtomove.co.uk

Goingtomove

Overall rating: ★ ★ ★

Classification:	Agency Portal	**Readability:**	★ ★ ★ ★
Updating:	Not Known	**Content:**	★ ★
Navigation:	★ ★ ★	**Speed:**	★ ★ ★

UK

The site, which is delivered by Legal & General, has access to a large independent network of estate agents.

There are six main areas within the website. The homepage has a quick search property portal, but it is best to proceed by the main property link to the left of the main tool bar.

The Property Site can be searched using minimum and maximum prices. Locations can be specified by county, and narrowed down by local area. Alternatively a search can be made by postcode.

The results are shown clearly with a good layout. With each result there is the opportunity to request full details, move immediately to the estate agent's website, to calculate the mortgage for the property and to contact a mortgage advisor.

The Estate Agents site enables the search function to locate estate agents by county and by local area. But there are some areas where estate agents are a bit thin on the ground.

The Mortgage Advisor site allows a similar search for advisors by postcode.

The Mortgage site shows a small but useful range of mortgages, some of which are declared to be exclusive to the mortgage advisors available on the site. By ticking the mortgage of most interest to you, and clicking the contact mortgage advisor button, you can bring together both a possible mortgage and an advisor.

The Surveyor site allows access to the 300 surveyors of the Legal & General surveying services nationwide.

SPECIAL FEATURES

The Mortgage Illustrator is a well laid out and is an easy-to-use tool. The variables you can utilise include deposit, repayment terms, interest rates and mortgage type. Additionally there is a 'How much can I borrow?' facility.

This site is very clear and easy to navigate. It is well worth a visit.

www.hol365.co.uk			
Homes-on-Line			
Overall rating: ★★★			
Classification:	Agency Portal	Readability:	★★★
Updating:	Daily	Content:	★★★
Navigation:	★★★	Speed:	★★★
UK			

Homes-on-Line was formed in 1996. Hol365 has been launched more recently. The site is devoted to buying, selling and owning a home. It not only gives access to property for sale, but also the full range of assistance you may require when purchasing a property. The site claims to have over 100,000 properties from over 1,000 estate agent's offices. You can arrange for viewings and registrations online with any of the estate agents and letting agents listed.

SPECIAL FEATURES

The wide range of options can be seen in the comprehensive list on the left hand side of the homepage.

Find a Home is the most important. Suitable properties can be located by feeding in area, price range and the number of bedrooms. The search results are shown with a brief description and a floor plan, but these are not always clear. However, a click on the address brings up a larger floor plan with a more detailed description. At this stage the estate agent is shown with contact details. You can register to receive regular property updates by Email if you wish.

What is my house worth? may sound useful but your details are merely passed to an estate agent to receive a valuation.

Finding an Estate Agent allows you to undertake a geographical search for agents.

OTHER FEATURES

You can advertise your own property on the website. The cost of the service is given to you when you have completed the application form, including some property details. The company indicates that some 180,000 people visit the site every month.

There is a range of other facilities on the site from legal to home improvements and home shopping.

This site is busy but repetitive. Your patience may run out before you get to the end.

www.homefile.co.uk
Homefile

Overall rating: ★ ★ ★			
Classification:	Real Estate	**Readability:**	★ ★ ★
Updating:	Not Known	**Content:**	★ ★ ★
Navigation:	★ ★ ★	**Speed:**	★ ★

UK

The site advertises itself as a comprehensive national database of properties and related services. It also contains a dedicated section on new homes. The site has freephone, Email and ring me connections.

SPECIAL FEATURES

The website has six main sub-sites.

The Property search site is comprehensive in that it covers buying, selling, letting, renting, short-term lettings and new homes. On the main buying site you can search comprehensively by county. And within a county you can search by local area. Alternatively, a search can be conducted by town or postcode. The search can be narrowed down within county and local area by price, property type, age of property, and the number of bedrooms.

When searching by location from the first page, all properties are shown, irrespective of price. Photographs, maps of the property locality and demographics are available. This produces a very comprehensive local picture. A variety of scales can be used on the maps, and each map frame carries a large range of ancillary services.

The site links to www.upmystreet.co.uk, which is reviewed in our Local Area section. The range of information produced is absolutely first class. Education, crime, health, etc. are all covered. At the end of this search you will have an excellent idea of the local area.

The New Homes section of Property search has a search facility by county only. Results are shown by development. All further information is through the appropriate building company.

The Finance site is the moneyworld.co.uk site that is reviewed in our broker section.

The Insurance section is a direct link to Letsure and exhibits a wide range of potential insurances for the homeowner.

The Legal Services link presents a live conveyancing service with online progress reports, 24 hours per day, seven days per week.

The Surveying and Valuation site has access to a network of fully qualified chartered surveyors.

The Don't Forget site contains a comprehensive range of local services. These include gas and electricity supply, local schools, home improvements, council tax, shops and amenities, removals and storage, car and van hire and other useful services.

This site is comprehensive and busy – perhaps too busy. But there is a lot there for the buyer.

www.homepages.co.uk
Homepages

Overall rating: ★★★★			
Classification:	Agency Portal	Readability:	★★★★
Updating:	Regularly	Content:	★★★★
Navigation:	★★★	Speed:	★★

UK

Homepages is an agency portal site belonging to infomediary MoneyeXtra (www.moneyextra.co.uk). It currently carries details of about 44,000 properties for sale through a large number of estate agencies listed on the site. Property rentals are delegated to Web2Let (www.web2let.co.uk).

You can initiate a property search at four levels:

* Quick Search, which only requires the location of the property.

* Search by location, price and number of bedrooms.

* Advanced search by location, price range, bedrooms/living rooms/bathrooms, keywords and recent listings.

*Meta Search across a number of property websites.

Advanced and Meta Searches are not posted on the homepage, unfortunately. You have to go into the Help area to find and access them. This should be your first point of call.

Properties are initially displayed with photographs and thumbnail sketches. Click on the photograph to access the full estate agency blurb. You can request further details by Email and put yourself on an alerts list. A mortgage illustration is displayed at 8% p.a. on 90% loan-to-value and you can commission a standard valuation, homebuyer's report or full building survey.

This area of the site contains valuable local information provided by the DfEE (primary and secondary schools and colleges, schools' results, house prices, council tax rates, surveyors, solicitors, removal firms and builders). You can call up a Multimap.com map of the area (with the property location circled) and an Environmental Risks Report by HomeCheck (www.homecheck.co.uk) covering flood, Radon, subsidence and landslip risks; proximity to coal mines, landfill sites and waste sites; air quality, contamination and pollution.

This site has improved greatly since last reviewed. It has a wider functionality and is altogether much faster. The only quibble is the absence of any reference to the Advanced and Meta Searches on the homepage.

www.home-sale.co.uk
Homesale

Overall rating: ★ ★ ★			
Classification:	Agency Portal	Readability:	★ ★ ★ ★
Updating:	Daily	Content:	★ ★ ★
Navigation:	★ ★ ★ ★	Speed:	★ ★ ★

UK

The Home-sale network is a national network of over 720 estate agents in the UK. All members are independent businesses as distinct from large chains. The site claims that this structure brings more commitment and greater insight into the process.

The Home-sale network is backed by Cendent Relocation plc. Every year the company helps some 100,000 families to move house as part of company relocation.

The opening page is clear and uncluttered and clearly shows the main sub-sites.

SPECIAL FEATURES

Find A Home opens with a map of the UK and the ability to select a county by way of a map, or by selecting from a drop-down table. Once selected, details on location, price range, and the minimum number of specified rooms can all be entered. The minimum distance from the town centre can also be specified.

By clicking on the Additional options button the searcher can inject a much wider range of options. This includes some twenty-two styles of property, eight options on type and six on the type of setting (village, rural etc.). Additionally age, parking, garden, heating and double-glazing are also features that can be included. In short, very full property requirements can be given.

Estate Agents can be selected by location. Full contact details are given, including Email addresses.

The Mortgage site links to directly to the What Mortgage site that we review later.

Moving and Advice is a very useful site with some good, common sense tips on selling and buying a house.

The site performs the main function well. Although purporting to represent a substantial number of agents, the site is a bit thin.

www.numberone4property.co.uk

Numberone4property

Overall rating: ★ ★ ★ ★

Classification:	Agency Portal	**Readability:**	★ ★ ★
Updating:	Daily	**Content:**	★ ★ ★ ★
Navigation:	★ ★ ★ ★	**Speed:**	★ ★ ★

UK

The site was established in 1997 and advertises itself as a totally independent site. They claim to have about 300,000 visits per month with their best day ever bringing in 11,000 site visitors.

The site claims to show about 50,000 properties. Although some individuals show their property, most of the properties are from estate agents. Some 50% are their own properties and some 50% from other sites.

Cover is strong in Scotland, Lancashire, Derby and Lincolnshire, with some in London.

The Homepage presents a property for sale entry point. Details of county, town or postcode can be entered. Once entry is gained there are three further options. All properties in that area can be viewed. The list can be qualified by entering a price range, or type of property or number of bedrooms. Additionally garage, central heating and double-glazing requirements can all be entered.

Search results are shown with a small photograph and basic details. Clicking on the address brings up more details with photographs. Links with estate agents are available.

Sometimes the links will take you into a completely new site.

SPECIAL FEATURES

New Homes has a simple search facility by county. But frequently you will be taken through to the builder's main site thus causing the necessity for another search.

The Estate Agents search is a simple search facility by county and town.

Local House Prices is a direct link to the Land Registry site. This site is excellent for house prices.

Homelocator is an Email facility that will be activated when a match is found for your housing requirements.

Neighbourhood Information offers an excellent range of comprehensive local information sites, all of which are reviewed in chapter four.

This site is sensibly laid out and contains a mine of information but it needs to develop more coverage.

www.primelocation.co.uk
Prime Location

Overall rating: ★ ★ ★

Classification:	Agency Portal	**Readability:**	★★★★
Updating:	Daily	**Content:**	★★★
Navigation:	★★	**Speed:**	★★

UK

Prime Location is owned by a group of estate agents and letting agents. They represent over 280 firms consisting of over 875 offices in London and across the country. The site is showing over 41,000 properties, of which some 30,000 are for sale and over 10,000 are for letting. The site offers all the help one would need to move, as well as details on financing.

The Homepage offers a start for buying process. The **buying** button on the top left hand list merely leads to a busy screen with a wide range of information. The **search for property** button on the homepage brings up the search screen.

The Homepage search allows you to insert up to three locations, property type, price range and the minimum and maximum number of bedrooms.

A well-laid out list of results allows you to move immediately to the property of interest. The options open are varied. You can view the full details, save the property in your own property file for later examination, open up an Email alert that will inform you of similar properties that satisfy your search criteria or contact the agent.

Unfortunately the request to view full details was not always successful.

Within the property search results the **Your Neighbourhood** button displays a wide range of local service that we review in chapter four. **Settling In** highlights some interesting aspects of getting to know your neighbours.

The **Selling** button on the left hand list brings up a screen of general interest articles.

The **Mortgage Tools** button uses the Charcol website which we review in chapter five.

There are some good things on this site. However, navigation and speed sometimes leave something to be desired.

www.propertyfinder.co.uk
Propertyfinder

Overall rating: ★ ★ ★ ★			
Classification:	Real Estate	**Readability:**	★ ★ ★ ★
Updating:	Daily	**Content:**	★ ★ ★ ★
Navigation:	★ ★ ★ ★	**Speed:**	★ ★ ★ ★

UK

The site was founded in 1995. In 2001 Asserta holdings acquired Property Finder. The claim is that the site has been repositioned as the site for premier properties. The site is now showing nearly 600 agents uploading from just over 800 offices.

The site is showing over 30,000 properties.

There is a facility to register your property requirements with the site, and you will be informed by Email of any matches.

The search process commences on the Homepage and is simple and straightforward. The initial search allows price range, number of bedrooms and the type of property and location to be entered. This can be entered by postcode, town or county. A map-search facility is preferred over post code or town. This allows a progressive narrowing down of the search area.

The search results are simple and well presented. There are plenty of options. Unfortunately, if the initial search is unsuccessful, on reversion to the search mode all initial information is lost. This causes unnecessary re-entering of the relevant data concerning the property.

Options available include more details, a request for more details to be sent, arranging a viewing, the ability to contact the estate agent and a location map. Additional photographs are also available.

The geographical search requests take into account duplicate place names throughout the country, and further refinement is possible.

Details of the properties vary widely. Room sizes are not always shown.

On the Homepage there is the facility to **Find an Agent**. The search results show both the estate agents and the number of properties they are showing.

A further useful addition on the Homepage is the **London Property Guide**. This gives a facility to search and locate properties and then to take an overview of that particular area. Transport, schools, price and types of property are all covered.

The **Selling** facility along the top tool bar is a simple search tool by post-code to produce a list of estate agents.

This is clearly one of the better sites. It concentrates on the essentials and is a must for every serious house-hunter.

www.propertylive.co.uk
Propertylive

Overall rating: ★ ★ ★			
Classification:	Agency Portal	Readability:	★★★★
Updating:	Daily	Content:	★★★
Navigation:	★★★★	Speed:	★★★

UK

The website is sponsored by The National Association of Estate Agents (NAEA) and there is an immediate link into the NAEA website by clicking the information button. The NAEA has in the region of 10,000 members. It is represented in more than 60% of estate agency offices in the UK.

The Homepage allows immediate access into the Quick Search facility. This offers an initial option of buying, renting, or of finding an estate agency. The initial quick search shows all the properties in the selected area in ascending price order. An impressive range of criteria that can be put into the quick search markedly improves the results. Photographs accompany each description, and there are Email links to the estate agency concerned.

Also available on the Homepage is the main Homes for Sale facility. By entering the data bank by this method you are immediately asked to identify the precise area that you wish to search. Property criteria are then entered. These include price, number of bedrooms and reception rooms, and options on garaging, central heating and freehold. The results are sorted either by price, location or distance to the city centre. Links are available to the appropriate estate agent.

SPECIAL FEATURES

Homes for Rent on the home page presents a similar series of options to the Homes for Sale.

Help with Moving Home, found on the homepage, offers a mixed range of services for both the public and the professional. There is also a further link to the NAEA website.

Terramedia Limited offers the facility to order aerial images of the area of interest. They cost £45 excluding VAT.

Npower offer access to a nationwide energy supply business.

The site presents a mix of content for both the public and professional. It is worth a visit by the home searcher.

www.property-platform.com
Property Platform

Overall rating: ★ ★ ★			
Classification: Agency Portal		**Readability:**	★ ★ ★
Updating: Six weeks		**Content:**	★ ★ ★
Navigation: ★ ★ ★		**Speed:**	★ ★ ★

UK

This is the site of The Guild of Professional Estate Agents. This is an association of independent estate agents who are brought together to facilitate widespread and effective marketing. The Guild is not a governing body in estate agency practise.

Properties are presented in a series of full colour, high quality magazines. These are available at no charge on the internet. Each magazine is produced every six weeks so new listings are never very far away from publication date. It claims that properties are marketed through nearly 400 independent estate agency offices. It maintains that each office is staffed by personnel with good local knowledge.

The Homepage immediately presents a Property Search. The initial search is quite simply by place or postcode, and whether you wish to buy or rent.

Perhaps not surprisingly this somewhat crude search provides a wide range of properties. These you can now further refine. The criteria that you can now feed in includes a search radius, minimum and maximum price and the number of bedrooms. But it is still not possible to specify the type of property you wish to purchase.

The results come with the highest price first. Each property has a photograph, and more information can be pulled down if required. The additional information is certainly comprehensive and includes room sizes. Area maps and area information are also available if required. The map is produced by **www.multimap.com** and the area information is provided by **www.upmysteet.com**.

SPECIAL FEATURES

The Sell & Let button takes you through a three-step procedure. Initially you enter the postcode of the property that you wish to sell, followed by full contact details and, finally, full details of the property. At the end of the third stage the details are sent to a member of the Guild.

The Portfolio button allows you to create a property portfolio and automate searches. Property details can be saved for quick reference, and notes can be added if you wish.

This is a useful site that is worth a visit. It is very simple to use.

www.property-seeker.co.uk
Property-seeker

Overall rating: ★ ★ ★ ★

Classification:	Agency Portal	Readability:	★★★★
Updating:	Daily	Content:	★★★★
Navigation:	★★★★	Speed:	★★★

UK

The site is also known as TMX. This is the Total Moving Experience. It has been set up by leading independent estate agents throughout the country to provide a comprehensive electronic solution to moving. The site is a service-led website designed to cover everything for the home and the home move. The site can also be accessed through **www.tmxhome.com**

It does not cost anything to buy through TMX. But when selling the local agent will arrange for interested buyers to view your property and on completion of the sale you will be responsible for the estate agents fee.

The Homepage reveals a top tool bar with some 11 major options. On the Homepage the Quick Homesearch button allows entry of town or postcode and from this a list of properties is displayed. The search results display brief details. But fuller details are available. Room sizes are well laid out and the total features available in the property are easy to see.

The **Quick Valuation** button, will excite interest, but unfortunately merely passes your details to a local estate agent for a visit.

The main **Homesearch** button reveals 12 major options. At this stage you begin to feel that you could get lost.

Property Search, accessed through Homesearch, allows you to enter a purchase price ceiling, number of bedrooms and property type. Search results appear in no particular order and initially show minimum detail. Further links offer full details. Monthly mortgage costs are shown, based on a 75% mortgage, over twenty-five years, and at 5% APR. Photographs and contact details are also available.

New Instructions enables you to keep up to date with the site by viewing the latest properties that have come on to the market. Two further facilities will allow you to view the properties attracting the most interest and those that have recently been reduced in price.

Back on the Homepage the **Finances** link takes you immediately into the mortgage page. A full range of **mortgage tools** is available, including quick quotes, a guide to mortgages, borrowing ability and a budget planner.

SPECIAL FEATURES

The **Mortgage** facility is excellent. It is an extremely comprehensive document. But the facility is only available to registered users. You will need to understand the mortgage market, but it does take almost everything into consideration and produces quick results.

From the Homepage, the **Legal** link displays conveyancers with the ability to participate in on-line conveyancing.

The **Services** link provides a very wide range of utility companies and tradesmen.

OTHER FEATURES

At the bottom of the Homepage there is a very useful function. After free registration you can pose questions to a number of professionals or tradesmen.

This is a comprehensive site. It is aptly named the total moving experience. But it is very busy and probably trying to do too much.

www.rightmove.co.uk
Rightmove

Overall rating: ★ ★ ★ ★ ★			
Classification:	Agency Portal	**Readability:**	★★★★★
Updating:	Not Known	**Content:**	★★★★★
Navigation:	★★★★	**Speed:**	★★★

UK

This is a site for estate agents to display their properties. The site makes an impressive mission statement at the beginning. It is to provide honest, clear and useful information. The site has recently been updated. It now includes auto-e-mail property updates, enhanced search capabilities and property details that can be printed directly from the site.

The site is jointly owned by four of the UK's biggest estate agency chains. They are Halifax, Countrywide Assured, Royal & Sun Alliance and Connell. Over half the top 100 estate agents use the site, covering 99% of UK postcodes. The majority of these homes are for sale. Viewing figures are significantly ahead of all the major rivals.

The site claims to offer the consumer a choice of over 30% of all residential properties on the market at any one time. Additionally they offer the ability to find the right property with three clicks of the mouse.

The Homepage contains the first move in the buying process. The same result is found in **Find a home** on the left hand tool bar or **Buying** on the top tool bar. The search starts with the entry of either location or postcode. This moves to the main search screen where type of property, distance from the central location, number of bedrooms and minimum and maximum values can be input.

Price bands vary. The size of the band increases as the price of the property increases. This is a clever feature and allows a more accurate response to search requests.

The search results are shown in descending price order. They come with a small description and links to the estate agent. By clicking on the location more detailed property descriptions are available, although for the most part room dimensions are not given.

A useful results summary and search parameters are displayed in the top left hand corner.

The **Selling** button brings up **Find an Agent**. This facility is excellent. It is extremely easy to use and the search results show a generous list of estate agents. Telephone details, fax details and Email communications are all included.

Both **Buying** and **Selling** sites contain useful guides.

This is a very good, uncluttered site. There is no advertising to distract visitors. For first time searchers, this is as good a place to start as anywhere. Five stars for simplicity and content.

www.smartestates.com
Smart Estates

Overall rating: ★ ★ ★			
Classification:	Agency Portal	**Readability:**	★ ★ ★ ★
Updating:	Daily	**Content:**	★ ★ ★ ★
Navigation:	★ ★ ★	**Speed:**	★ ★ ★

UK

The site is a mixture of open market properties and new homes. An immediate benefit is that your previous searches are automatically recorded and available to you when you return.

The site is showing some 70,000 properties, the majority of which are for sale. Some 1,600 agents are uploading properties to the site. There are some 7,000 new homes available for inspection.

The **Find Property** button enables us to locate **Residential Search**. This starts with town selection. Then follows types of property. There are over 15 to select from and is certainly one of the most comprehensive lists on the web.

Prior to presenting the properties the searcher is offered the ability to set up their own Smart Page. Personal details are required. You will be able to see details of your last ten searches. Additionally you can see if properties that match your requirements have been removed or added to the database.

The properties are presented with some good general information and a photograph. The initial results offer options including more details, shortlist, request information and a mortgage quote. The quality of the additional details is variable.

The **New Homes** section is similarly laid out. But additionally there is a section for selection by developer. This presents a list of over 50 builders. Some well known and some not so well-known.

The site is comprehensive in that it offers a wide range of options and services. But the **Mortgage** facility is disappointing. It merely gives an option for the sort of mortgage advisor the searcher might require and then a list in the appropriate locality.

Find a Professional will prove to be of benefit to those about to move. It provides a list of nearly 60 services that might be needed, together with a location search.

This is a reasonable site for property. It is worth a visit. But don't expect it to be user friendly.

www.thisislondon.co.uk
This is London

Overall rating: ★ ★ ★			
Classification:	Agency Portal	**Readability:**	★ ★ ★
Updating:	Daily	**Content:**	★ ★
Navigation:	★ ★ ★	**Speed:**	★ ★

UK

This is London is a composite site describing many facets of London. One of the main sections is **Homes**. The site claims to show over nearly 90,000 properties across London and the south-east.

The opening page of **Property Search** presents a screen for both buying and renting. Parameters required are location details, the minimum and maximum price, type of property, and the minimum number of bedrooms. Most properties are presented with photographs. Fuller details are available if required, and there is an email link to the estate agent.

The information page submitted for further details only has to be completed once per visit.

The search for rentals works in a similar fashion except minimum rental requirements are entered.

Property News offers a rather mixed bag of routine tips and gossip.

A recent innovation is that the site will now Email you immediately if a suitable property goes to market. If your search is unsuccessful, you can simply sign up to the

Homes by Email service. Details can be sent to you either daily or weekly, whichever is more convenient.

Letting is possible on the site. You can advertise your property for letting for a £5 fee for a fourteen-day advertisement.

The **Message Boards** provide a public forum for a whole range of property topics.

www.vebra.com			
Vebra			
Overall rating: ★ ★ ★ ★			
Classification: Agency Portal		**Readability:**	★ ★ ★ ★
Updating: Daily		**Content:**	★ ★ ★
Navigation: ★ ★ ★ ★		**Speed:**	★ ★ ★
UK			

Vebra claim to be the largest provider of estate agency software in the UK. They have a customer base of over 1,600 offices.

The Homepage gives entry immediately to a **Quicksearch** facility that includes **UK Homes for Sale** and **UK Homes To Let**. It also includes a **UK Commercial and French** section.

The **Property Search** section allows the input of minimum and maximum price, number of bedrooms and two regions. However, it does not allow you to select the type of property.

Results show the whole of the region selected. The properties in each major town are shown and are refined when you select areas and towns of interest. Properties ascend in price range, and most have a photograph. Options include **Go to Agent**, **Full Details** and **Add to Basket**.

UK Property leads to the same screen as **Quicksearch**. Both contain **UK Homes to Let**. Rental is requested by minimum and maximum price per week and bedrooms required.

The site is worth a visit; however, it would be helpful to be able to select the type of property desired.

Other Property Websites

Bamboo Avenue
www.bambooavenue.com

The site passes on your property requirements to all the estate agents in the area where you are hoping to buy. There is a charge based on the number of agents in each area. The site also covers mortgages and finance, removals and storage and solicitors and surveys.

County Web Property Locator
www.propertylocator.co.uk

There are less than 1,000 properties on this site. A figure of nearly 300 estate agents is suggested as contributing to the site. The search is by region and price and includes buying and renting. A list of estate agents is provided but coverage is patchy.

Homes on View
www.homesonview.co.uk

There are few frills on this site. The site claims 29,000 properties and 490 agents. The only function is the search engine.

It is possible to register your requirements to automatically receive Email notification of any new properties. Home search is by location, maximum and minimum prices and number of bedrooms. There is a full list of estate agents.

Homes-UK
www.homes-uk.co.uk

The site claims to have on average 4,000 UK houses for sale. It is also possible on this site to enter your own property details for viewing by both the public and estate agents. The details can be viewed online for up to three months.

The property search allows for additional features such as garage, central heating and double-glazing.

Partake
www.partake.co.uk

The site operates a simple system. A potential buyer merely lets the site know what they are looking for and the specific requirements will be sent to over 13,600 estate agents.

The site is certainly a time-saver and is worth an examination. There is an indemnity against failed transactions.

Property World
www.propertyworld.co.uk

The site offers a number of facilities including a property search, links to estate agents and the ability to find experts and services.

The property search mechanism is certainly not the easiest to use and at times gets frustrating. However, there is a full range of options to assist in the search itself.

www.thegoodwebguide.co.uk 37

Pure Property
www.pureproperty.com

The site has been created using the latest technology by estate agents. It does not have any banner advertisements or links to financial services. It is purely property. The results of the searches come directly from the agent's websites.

The site is showing over 35,000 properties, the majority of which are concentrated in London and the surrounding areas. Approximately 70% of the property is for sale. Nearly 200 offices are uploading property details.

The graphics are excellent. The site is worth a visit.

The House Hunter
www.thehousehunter.co.uk

The site has a range of functions other than just a property search. It is interactive. It contains buyer and seller guides, as well as property features and a range of property-related professional services. The nationwide property search is by price and number of bedrooms. The site is worth a visit.

The National Property Register
www.national-property-register.co.uk

In addition to the search facility by geography and price, the site offers other services. There is an invitation to submit a buyer's registration form. Your details will be sent to all registered agents. They will send details of those properties that are suitable.

Individuals can add their property to the site for free. There is a link to the Land Registry for price details. Additionally there is a mortgage calculator.

BBC Good Homes
www.bbc.co.uk/rightmoves

As one would expect the BBC has produced a useful and informative property site. Notwithstanding this it is not an easy site to use. Once into the site click on 'How to buy online', and then move to property search. Properties are from Estate Agents and Builders. It is certainly worth a visit, if only for the ancillary information.

Ezi2buy Property Consultants
www.ezi2buy.co.uk

The site serves only Home Buyers. They state that until recently all residential real estate agents and brokers represented the sellers, a fact lost on many home-buyers.

They now claim a new breed of broker has emerged to work for them. The claim is that the buyer pays no more for the services of a buyer's agent than he or she would if using a traditional seller's agent.

Specialist Property Sites

OVERSEAS PROPERTY

Worldwide
www.tiscali.co.uk

Tiscali has its base in Italy. The site merged in July 2001. It now provides services to some 16 million registered users in 15 countries. The site appears to deal with everything but property. However, in the search box type in 'Int'l Property' and nearly 60 sites of varying descriptions will appear. Many sites are in Europe, but there are also sites in America, the West Indies, Bermuda and the Channel Islands. From these sites you can log on to even more sites. It has to be worth a visit.

Europe
www.epn.es

The site is located in Spain. It claims that it is not an estate agent but a property listing service. Their aim is to provide an easy-to-use search engine where estate agents and private sellers from all over Europe can list their properties for sale or rent.

The search function is quick and easy to use and reveals properties located worldwide. Although the majority are in Spain (over 1,000). Details on the properties are impressive, and photographs are available. Most welcome is the simple, but remarkably efficient, currency converter. This is a good site.

Spain
www.spanish-property-online.com

This site is exactly the same as www.overseaspropertyonline. com. The site seems to have everything; it doesn't really want to tell you too much about itself.

Notwithstanding this, the site not only provides information across a wide geographical range in Spain, but there are numerous sections that are particularly relevant to the Spanish home-seeker. These include a section on buying property, the weather and mortgages. There are many others. Even the pets have a section.

The properties come with a brief description and good photographs. Personal details are required both for further information and details of similar properties. However, the site is a must for potential property owners in Spain.

COUNTRY AND WATERSIDE PROPERTIES/PROPERTIES WITH LAND

www.ruralscene.co.uk

The site claims to maintain a portfolio of approximately 150 properties with land. The range of properties shown is considerable and includes commercial farms, small holdings and equestrian properties.

The search is by geographical area. It is quick, and the results come with a good description and photograph.

www.farmsearch.co.uk

This is a specialist website for those seeking farms, estates, agricultural, rural and sporting facilities. The search facilities are impressive, as is the degree of categorisation on the site. Search is by region or county, and there are over 20 types of farm or outdoor facility listed in the search lists.

There is a wanted section for those wishing to advertise for a farm, land or estate within the UK. There is a small charge for this.

There is plenty of information on this site and it should be explored by anyone who dreams of making for the outdoors.

www.equusproperty.co.uk

Equus specialises in country and equestrian properties throughout Kent, Sussex, Surrey and Hampshire. The site states that the properties displayed represent only a small selection of the range of country and equestrian properties for sale with Equus.

The properties shown on the site are at the top-end of the market.

www.humberts.co.uk

Humberts is a firm of national Chartered Surveyors and Estate Agents with experience in country houses, farms and estates. The price range of some of their country houses start at under £100,000!

In the Rural Section there is a wide selection of properties available. This is a useful site for a wide range of people.

Additional sites in this category:

www.watersideproperties.co.uk
www.mayfairoffice.co.uk
www.countrylife.co.uk

UNUSUAL PROPERTIES
www.property.org.uk

This site for unusual properties is unusual itself. The homepage mentions a wide range of unusual buildings. These include castles, islands, houseboats, Martello towers, churches, schools, windmills, watermills, pubs and barns. There is certainly enough here to whet the appetite, but most of the information is only available to members. So the enthusiast must pay a modest £10 per annum for access.

PERIOD PROPERTY

www.periodproperty.co.uk

This site is exactly what it says: it is for people with a passion for period property. There are over 250 properties on the site. A range of other services is offered including a discussion forum, information and products and services. This is a site for the true enthusiast.

SELF-BUILD/ SEARCHING FOR PLOTS

www.buildstore.co.uk

This site is designed to be the one-stop navigator for the UK self-build and renovation market.

It contains the site Plotsearch at **www.plotsearch.co.uk**. This links back to Buildstore. The standard lifetime subscription to Plotsearch is £39.

MOBILE HOMES
www.ukmobilehomes.com

This site provides numerous links to information on a wide range of subjects connected to the mobile home lifestyle.

LOFTS

www.manloft.co.uk

The site advertises itself as part of London's cultural restoration. It has both a residential and 'mixed' development but properties are very thin on the ground.

www.urbanspaces.co.uk

The company purports to be the ultimate website in loft living and contemporary design.

TIMESHARE

www.timeshare.org.uk

This is the website for the Timeshare Consumers Association. It contains a wealth of information concerning timeshare and a list of recommended resellers. Everyone getting involved in timeshare should visit this site.

HOLIDAY SWAP SITES

www.holi-swaps.com	More than 10,000 members in nearly 70 countries.
www.holswap.com	Three month free listing when you join up.
www.gti-home-exchange.com	Membership starts at £20.

Regional sites

Regional sites can be accessed directly through local estate agents, which can be found in the websites listed in the next section. Here is a list of some regional websites. London, because of its size, also merits a mention under regions.

SCOTLAND

www.aspc.co.uk	Aberdeen Solicitors Centre.
www.bspcbricks.co.uk	Borders Solicitors Property Centre.
www.dgspc.co.uk	Dumfries & Galloway Solicitors Property Centre.

www.espc.co.uk	Edinburgh Solicitors Property Centre.
www.f-kspc.co.uk	Fife & Kinross Solicitors Property Centre.
www.gspc.co.uk	Glasgow Solicitors Property Centre.
www.hspc.co.uk	Highland Solicitors Property Centre.
www.nespc.com	North East Solicitors Property Centre.
www.pspc.co.uk	Perthshire Solicitors Property Centre.
www.spcmoray.com	Moray Solicitors Property Centre.
www.sspc.co.uk	Scottish Solicitors Property Centre.
www.tspc.co.uk	Tayside Solicitors Property Centre.

WALES

www.propertyfinderwales.co.uk	Portal site for estate agents in Wales.
www.property-wales.co.uk	One-stop portal for Wales.
www.robbie-howarth.co.uk	Homes for sale or rent in North Wales.
www.thishouseisforsale.co.uk	Estate agents and new houses in Wales.

NORTHERN IRELAND

www.niproperty.net	A complete property portal for NI.
www.antrim-properties.com	Limited properties. Contact details.
www.housesinteractive.com	About 20 estate agents around NI.
www.nipropertysales.com	Limited properties. DIY selling.
www.propertyat.com	Estate Agents in NI.
www.propertynews.com	Claims 90% of agents and 12,000 properties.

LONDON

www.ealinghomes.co.uk	Ealing and other areas.
www.excelproperty.co.uk	Buying and renting in London.
www.findaproperty.com	Reviewed under main websites.
www.homenetuk.com	London and the South East.
www.hotproperty.co.uk	London and the South-east.
www.londonhomenet.com	Sales, lettings and flat shares.
www.londonproperties.co.uk	London Area.
www.londonpropertyguide.co.uk	Sales and EAs in Greater London.
www.lpn.co.uk	London Property News.
www.propertycity.com	London resource.
www.propertydirect.co.uk	London and the South East.

www.propertymartonline.com	East London and West Essex.
www.propertymatters.co.uk	Docklands property specialists.
www.propertywiz.co.uk	Residential sales across London.
www.salesandlettings.com	London and the South East.
www.tudorpark.com	Specialists in SE London.
www.wa-ellis.co.uk	Properties in inner-west and SW London.
www.wimbledonproperty search.co.uk	Wimbledon area.

How to find an Estate Agent

The National Association of Estate Agents
www.naea.co.uk

The National Association of Estate Agents has in the region of 10,000 members. Through its members it represents more than 60% of estate agency offices in the UK.

Entry to the agent search facility is by way of 'General Public'. The results are published by individual name and then agency. Links are available to the agents.

The Independent Association of Estate Agents
www.mortgageseekers.co.uk

This is a public service site on behalf of the Independent Association of Estate Agents. The site is reviewed in full under Mortgage Brokers (chapter 5).

The search facility is at the bottom of the homepage. Only a location need be entered.

Links are available to the estate agents, as is a free enquiry service to let them know your requirements.

National Directory of Estate Agents
www.ukpropertyshop.co.uk

The National Directory of Estate Agents and Letting Agents covers 18,000 agents in 3,000 towns. The search is simple. It will locate the agents in any town or postcode. Access is through the agent's own website to view the properties available.

The Yellow Pages
www.yell.com

Yellow Pages are well known. Their simple format is just as simple on the net. The only requirement is to type in estate agents and location or postcode. Addresses and telephone numbers are given.

Each result comes with a map and directions; however, links to the estate agent are not available.

The site represents The National Directory of Estate Agents. It is for use by any private individual looking to buy or rent residential property. It aims to list every office of every residential estate agent or letting agent in the UK.

www.thegoodwebguide.co.uk **43**

www.ukpropertyshop.com
UK Property Shop

Overall rating: ★ ★ ★ ★

Classification:	National Directory	**Readability:**	★★★★★
Updating:	Daily	**Content:**	★★★★★
Navigation:	★★★★★	**Speed:**	★★★★★

UK

UK Property Shop claims to be a unique directory of estate agents and letting agents. It covers some 18,000 offices in 3,000 towns across the United Kingdom.

The process is extremely simple. You start by finding all the agents you require in a particular town, and then simply use their websites to give you access to the property for sale or rent.

The site itself does not carry listings of properties for sale or to rent, either on behalf of estate agents or private individuals. It is purely a directory of estate agents.

The Homepage gives you immediate access to the main search buttons. One is for **Property for Sale** and one is **Property to Rent**.

Click on **Property for Sale** and a simple screen asks you to enter the town or postcode to find all the estate agents. There is a separate button for **London Estate Agents**.

The search results are clear and arrive quickly. You can click on the links to agent's websites to see current property for sale.

Additionally there is a free enquiry service. You can inform the estate agent of the kind of property that you are seeking.

Multiple applications are not required. One simple form can be completed and the site will email this to all the estate agents you have selected with a simple tick box. Within any one town it is possible to narrow the search to a particular area.

London Estate Agents are handled on their own. The searcher can select from London districts. Over 100 separate districts are shown. This allows good geographical selection to be exercised.

Property to Let is handled in exactly the same way as **Property for Sale**. It is quick, clear and precise.

This is an excellent directory site, and it would be madness not to use the facility. It will take a lot of the hassle out of searching for property.

Estate Agents

Some of the larger chains of estate agents show their properties on sites already reviewed in the main property websites section. Below are some of the major estate agency sites worth looking at.

www.teamprop.co.uk
The TEAM Association

Overall rating: ★ ★ ★

Classification:	Agency Portal	Readability:	★ ★
Updating:	Not Known	Content:	★ ★ ★
Navigation:	★ ★ ★ ★	Speed:	★ ★ ★

UK

Estate Agency News includes TEAM in their league table, where it sits comfortably in the top ten. The site has been active since 1966. The charts show it as having over 500 members showing over 20,000 properties.

They claim that the ability to multi-list properties means that every home for sale through a TEAM estate agent is available at every TEAM office through the country.

The **Property Search** function is by area or agent. County and town can be selected. Properties are offered in price bands, with the number of properties available. The search results lead to a full description, photograph and links to the estate agent. A search by **Agent** produces a list of agents available in your area of interest.

A useful site with a good spread of agents.

www.marketplace.co.uk
Bradford & Bingley

Overall rating: ★ ★ ★

Classification:	Estate Agent	Readability:	★ ★
Updating:	Daily	Content:	★ ★ ★
Navigation:	★ ★ ★ ★	Speed:	★ ★

UK

The Bradford & Bingley site is very comprehensive indeed. It offers much more than just property as there is a huge amount of information on the site. Certainly the site is very busy. The number of estate agencies is nearly 400

The **Property Search** function begins with a search by city, town or village. Alternatively, you can use the first part of a postcode. Both are very efficient. The map search simply magnifies the map thus enabling you to narrow the search to town or city. The search is quick and a list of properties in the area is displayed with photograph, price and some basic details. Further information is available, together with the relevant branch telephone number.

Prior to commencing the search there is a choice of either properties currently in Bradford & Bingley agencies, or the wider market. The wider-market properties are shown by Rightmove, reviewed in the main property section.

The **Residential Lettings and Management** does not have the same coverage and the search is a disappointing hit-and-miss affair.

This is a busy site and it is easy to get distracted.

www.yourmove.co.uk
Norwich Union

Overall rating: ★ ★ ★

Classification:	Estate Agents	**Readability:**	★ ★ ★
Updating:	Daily	**Content:**	★ ★ ★
Navigation:	★ ★ ★ ★	**Speed:**	★ ★

UK

The Your Move site is the estate agency division of Norwich Union. There are 340 branches throughout the UK, and the site is showing 16,000 properties. The site contains numerous other features including a **mortgage calculator, guides to buying and selling your house, insurance solutions,** and **surveys and conveyancing.**

The **Property Search** opens with either a map selection or a selection of up to three regions from drop down lists. Then follows the ability to select up to four branches from the area that you wish to view. The theory is good, but only applies if there are enough branches on the ground in your area of interest.

A further refinement allows closer geographical selection within the town concerned. Finally, property type, minimum and maximum price and number of bedrooms required are entered.

The results come with price, photograph and some basic details. There is also the ability to request further information.

A workmanlike site that does what is asked of it.

www.reedsrains.co.uk
Reeds Rains

Overall rating: ★ ★ ★

Classification:	Estate Agents	**Readability:**	★ ★ ★
Updating:	Daily	**Content:**	★ ★ ★
Navigation:	★ ★ ★	**Speed:**	★ ★ ★

UK

Reed Rains has been selling properties since 1868. Their area of business activity is the North of England as far south as Staffordshire and North Wales. The agency has 138 estate agents offices.

The **Property Search** opens with either a **Quicksearch** by postcode or a geographical search from a map. The latter is clear and precise and allows for a further selection of the nearest district or town. But you will need to know your geography. Minimum and maximum prices, together with the required number of bedrooms, can be entered. The results come with photographs and some good descriptions. A location map and further details are available.

Quicksearch is exactly that. Enter a postcode, county, town or area and the results appear with surprising speed.

There is a section on **Prestige Property** and **Lettings.**

The **Mortgage section** is thin and concludes with a telephone number or an Email to Reeds Rains.

A good site for the North of England and worth a visit.

Other Estate Agency Chains

Arun Estates
www.arunestates.co.uk

Arun Estates is a privately run property group. It operates a network of approximately 125 estate agents across the South East of England. The company was formed in 1991 when it acquired over 100 estate agencies from Prudential Assurance. The Group operates through a number of different trading names throughout the south-east. The names include Wyatts, Pittis, Wyatt & Son, Cubitt & West, Ward & Partners and Douglas Allen Spiro. Each part of the group runs its own website which can be accessed through Arun Estates.

Hamptons International
www.hamptons.co.uk

There are nearly sixty offices nationwide. This is a comprehensive site. It offers quality properties across Southern England. The property search is very quick and easy to use. The site also offers a wide range of services.

Chancellors Estate Agents
www.chancellors.co.uk

The Chancellors Group of Estate Agents is independent with fifty-five offices in Southern England and Wales. Trading is under Chancellors in The Home Counties and Oxfordshire, Ainscombe & Ringland in London and Middlesex and Russell Baldwin & Bright in Herefordshire and mid-Wales.

Kinleigh, Folkard & Hayward
www.kfh.co.uk

Offices are located primarily in London and the Home Counties. This includes Kent, Surrey, Middlesex and Hertfordshire. The site offers a wide range of services and property.

Directory Sites for Builders and New Homes

There are two main directory sites for listing builders of new homes. These we review briefly below. On the following pages we list the major builders in the UK and review the ten largest websites. We complete the section with a list of all the major builders in the UK, together with their websites.

Smart New Homes
www.smartnewhomes.com

Smart New Homes is a leading site dedicated to the new homes industry. Over 50 builders are listed on the site. To access all the information there is a requirement to log onto the site.

The New Home Finder enables the searcher to search by Town and Country or by choosing a New Home Builder. The former is a comprehensive national directory including all the locations that have developments.

When selecting the type of property there are over 30 selections. This enables the searcher to focus closely on his own requirements. The site is showing some 70,000 new and second hand properties across the UK.

This is a good site for the new home seeker.

New Homes
www.new-homes.co.uk

This website, launched in March 2002, promotes new homes for sale. The site states that there are over 150,000 new houses, flats or retirement homes on the site. Purchasers have to put in the minimal amount of property information and the site returns brief details of developments meeting the criteria. Selection of one of the developments takes the potential purchaser directly to the related page of the house builder's website.

There is the facility to store search results from any location to peruse at a later date.

This new site has an air of maturity about it. It represents an absolute must for those considering the purchase of a new house.

Major House Builders Websites

These builders represent the largest house builders in the UK. This is measured by housing turnover. The figures are produced by *Building Magazine*.

www.wimpey.co.uk			
Wimpey			
Overall rating: ★ ★ ★ ★			
Classification:	Builder	**Readability:**	★ ★ ★
Updating:	Not Known	**Content:**	★ ★ ★ ★
Navigation:	★ ★ ★ ★	**Speed:**	★ ★ ★ ★
UK			

According to *Building Magazine* Wimpey has the largest housing turnover in the UK. This site gives immediate access to both Wimpey and McClean Homes.

The new home seeker should move direct to the Wimpey **Homes** button on the left-hand tool bar. On the first page, click on **Nationwide search** in the centre of the screen.

From here you can select a region by clicking the map of the United Kingdom. But if you know the name of the development you can select it by typing in the first few letters of the site.

The map option is clear and speedy. The area selected presents a more detailed breakdown by counties enclosed within the larger area. After selecting a county you can enter a price range and the number of bedrooms. The search is further narrowed by use of a **town** button.

At this stage if the results of your search are negative you may be directed to McClean Homes, if they have locations that meet the criteria.

But there is a degree of frustration in this sort of search. You may just want to live in a particular county, yet you have to go through all of the towns and may receive negative results.

It is probably better to search by development site as the drop-down list comes with the town attached to the development.

Once located you can connect to the location and the area in detail by way of a map. Descriptions are available, as well as full interactive details. Links will take you to **specifications, walkthrough** and **floorplans**.

Walkthrough is disappointing as the rooms were not shown as well as one might have expected. But the **floorplans** are clear and precise.

The **How to find us map,** with directions, is excellent.

The site for McClean Homes follows exactly the same search format.

Although not perfect, this is just the site you would expect to see from the UK's leading house builder.

www.barratthomes.co.uk
Barratt

Overall rating: ★ ★ ★			
Classification:	Builder	Readability:	★★★★
Updating:	Not Known	Content:	★★
Navigation:	★★★★	Speed:	★★★★

UK

Barratt has been building homes since 1958. They have over 300 developments throughout the UK. Their developments range from studio apartments from £40,000 to 7-bedroom homes from £2.5 million.

The **Location Search** shows a map of the United Kingdom. From here you select the appropriate region. The search narrows as you can now click on **County**. From here you can see the developments, either underway or projected. By positioning the pointer you can see the precise location from a pop-up icon. This is a good search facility.

A picture of the development, with description and a map is then made available. The map can be enlarged.

However, the information does not include such basics as floor plans, or an outline of the development itself. Some of the developments had clearly not been started and you are merely invited to request a brochure.

The **Brochure request** button enables yo to register your personal details and the type of property you are looking for. You can specify a maximum of five developments from within one area.

Buying Made Easy concerns an offer for the new homebuyer to reserve a Barratt home. Within seven days after an independent valuation, they will make you a fair offer on your own property. The information states that part-exchange is normally available within each division's operating area. This is on selected sites and selected properties. Barratt reserves the right to decide whether or not properties are acceptable for the service.

Other facilities offered the new-home buyer include a **First Time Buyer** service.

The search facility is good. But the detailed property information presented to the searcher could be better.

www.bryant.co.uk
Taylor Woodrow

Overall rating: ★ ★ ★			
Classification:	Builder	**Readability:**	★ ★ ★
Updating:	Not Known	**Content:**	★ ★ ★ ★
Navigation:	★ ★	**Speed:**	★ ★ ★

UK

Bryant Homes and Taywood Homes are part of the Taylor Woodrow Group.

The site opens immediately with **Homefinder Quick Search**. Selection is by type of property and geography. The UK is divided into four regions.

The results are comprehensive. A map appears with the full range of developments. All are colour coded. Adjacent charts of the appropriate colour link up to the numbered developments. A further colour coding shows those sites that match your requirements and those that are considered capable of selection. The presentation is clever and easy to read.

Unfortunately, there is not a great deal of detail available. The selected developments can be indicated by box ticking, and a brochure can be requested.

But the **Quick Search** is something of a red herring as it is better to go immediately from the Homepage via **Homefinder**. This presents better search parameters by allowing a more discrete description of your property requirements. These include the number of bedrooms, type of property, approximate price range and expected move dates. Notwithstanding this the results are handled just the same as with **Quick Search**.

Again, maps can be viewed and brochures requested, but it is difficult to get anything on the screen that adds significantly to an understanding of the property.

Local information is provided by **www.upmystreet.com**, which is reviewed in chapter four.

SPECIAL FEATURES

Switch to Lifestyles Homes reveals developments of Taywood Lifestyle Homes. These are age exclusive. The principal owner has to be over a certain age, say 50 or 60. The properties are located close to local amenities. Security and managed grounds are included.

Your Move reveals a **Bryant House Buying Guide** taking you through seven steps of the buying process

Bryant Design is more interesting as this allows you to browse through their online catalogue. There may be a feeling of overkill here. After opening up 'Kitchens' you are invited to choose from over 50 different designs of unit finish! But the items are well displayed and soon begin to take your interest. Certainly anyone committing to the purchase of a new home will spend many happy hours here.

This is a good solid site that is well worth a visit.

www.persimmonhomes.com			
Persimmon			
Overall rating: ★ ★			
Classification:	Builder	**Readability:**	★ ★ ★
Updating:	Not Known	**Content:**	★ ★
Navigation:	★ ★ ★	**Speed:**	★ ★

Persimmon Homes has recently acquired Beazer Homes.

The **Homefinder** initial page had plenty of options. A search can be made by **County** and **Price Range** for a wide search, or by **Town/City** and **Price Range** for a narrow search. The number of bedrooms can be entered.

The search by **County** and **Price Range** is just what it proclaims to be, but it may be better to go to **Town/City**. The site, however, is slow returning to Home, and if a search has been unsuccessful the initial information is not retained. It must be re-entered and this can be rather laborious.

Information is not always available, and there is a **Send me a brochure** button and a **Call me** button.

The search by site enables you to search on site name only. Unfortunately the site name does not come with a corresponding location, and thus another laborious trawl is required through all the sites.

The results come with little more information than would be received from a poor estate agent. The map is not of high quality, and the photographs could be improved. The image

www.thegoodwebguide.co.uk **51**

can be enlarged, but it added nothing to the site. No floor plans were available.

This is one of the largest builders in the UK.

www.berkeleyhomes.co.uk
Berkeley Homes

Overall rating: ★ ★ ★ ★ ★

Classification:	Real Estate New Homes	Readability:	★ ★ ★ ★
Updating:	Not Known	Content:	★ ★ ★ ★
Navigation:	★ ★	Speed:	★ ★ ★ ★

UK

Berkeley Homes mean business. That is the impression you get from the opening screen. You are immediately presented with a **Quick Search** facility. Here you can tell the site exactly what you are looking for. The search is quick and effective and gets you into the right mood straight away. It even tells you if all the plots are reserved.

The **Keyword** search allows you to enter your precise requirements. A four bedroom house in Milton Keynes would be an example

The **Find Your New Home** button shows that the main area of interest of Berkeley Homes is the south-east of England. The area is defined by a line from Cambridgeshire to Dorset. A clear county map is shown and you merely click on the desired county.

The available properties are shown in a small presentation box and by selecting the appropriate development further details present themselves. A 360-degree virtual tour is available. The loading is quick and the panoramic view is comprehensive and satisfying. You can quickly switch from one view to another. This feature is exactly what prospective purchasers require.

Additional information includes **full details, floor plans, site plans** and **location details**. Clear and concise general specifications are also shown.

Local information is available through links to **www.upmystreet.com**. This site is reviewed in chapter four

The **Customer Services** site gives details of the **Underwritten Part Exchange scheme** where you can reserve your new home before you have sold your present house. **Berkeley Homes Optional Services** reveals what is available in terms of options in your new home. These options include electrical, plumbing, kitchen units, worktops, floor finishes and colours

This is an excellent site. Just what the searcher requires on a wet Sunday afternoon. Five stars for consistency.

---

www.wilsonbowden.plc.uk
Wilson Bowden

Overall rating: ★ ★ ★

Classification:	Builder	**Readability:**	★ ★
Updating:	Not Known	**Content:**	★ ★ ★
Navigation:	★ ★ ★	**Speed:**	★ ★

UK

Wilson Bowden's house building operation spans more than 30 counties across England and Wales. Together with a recently established business in Scotland, it operates under the name of David Wilson Homes Ltd. This company operates largely at the upper-end of the housing market with some 65% of the developments being four, five and six bedroom houses.

Wilson Bowden City Homes is a new division of Wilson Bowden plc. This site has been launched to address the increasing demands for city centre living. These two sites may best be entered through **www.dwh.co.uk** and **www.wbcityhomes.co.uk**

David Wilson Homes Ltd is entered through the icon on the right hand tool bar. The property search starts through the **Homefinder** on the top tool bar. A selection by county, type of property, price range and number of bedrooms is available. Unfortunately the **Search again** button clears all of the original information and all selection criteria have to be entered again.

The search results are clear and come with plot information, site details and the ability to request a brochure.

The site details give full directions and includes information on education, health, services, shopping, sport and transport.

When the results have been revealed the **Interior features** and **Exterior features** along the top tool bar are a limited showcase for the company. They add little to the search. Certainly floor layouts and some virtual tours would have made the site more interesting. As it is, it seems that the brochure reigns supreme.

Wilson Bowden City Homes opens with a map of the UK with an invitation to open **Locations**. The next map enables you to identify the locations where developments are taking place or are proposed. When opened basic details are given of each development or proposed development. Contact details are also given.

This is a moderate site. The lack of hard information is disappointing.

www.bellway.co.uk			
Bellway			
Overall rating: ★ ★ ★ ★			
Classification:	Builder	**Readability:**	★ ★ ★
Updating:	Not Known	**Content:**	★ ★ ★ ★
Navigation:	★ ★ ★	**Speed:**	★ ★

UK

Bellway Homes has been in existence for over 50 years. It is active in nearly every part of the country. It builds across the housing spectrum from small apartments to large detached luxury homes.

They have exceeded in selling over 5,700 homes in a single year. The business today is amongst the top five volume house builders in the UK.

The entry to the site certainly looks exciting. You can take a look at homes across the UK, request a brochure, or take a virtual tour of their homes.

The map display is easy to navigate, with large recognisable regions that are well illustrated. Following selection of region, current developments are presented with address, type of property and links. The links take you to exactly what the house searcher is looking for. **House types, floor plans, specifications, area maps with directions**, and **site layout** are all there.

Dimensions are shown in both metric and imperial units. And additionally there is information on **education** and **amenities**. The presentation of information is excellent.

It is possible to have a virtual tour of Bellway Homes. It is accessed from the Homepage but to view the images you need to download the plug-in from IPIX (**www.ipix-eu.com**).

Bellway Bespoke is entered from the Homepage and offers a range of optional extras that can personalise the new home. These can range from bathroom and kitchen colours through to conservatories.

There is also a facility for Bellway Homes to take your current property in part exchange. Negotiations for this have to take place at site level.

A good site with some excellent information on their developments.

www.laing.com
John Laing Homes

Overall rating: ★ ★ ★ ★

Classification:	Builder	Readability:	★★★★
Updating:	Not Known	Content:	★★★★
Navigation:	★★	Speed:	★★★★

UK

Laing Homes Group is a division of John Laing. It is one of the UK's premier housing developers with operations in London, the South East and the Midlands. The Group celebrated its 150th anniversary in 1998. The impressive array of awards over the years can be seen in the **Awards** section of **About Us**.

Laing Homes develop around 1,300 houses per year. The new houses range from starter homes to executive family homes.

The company also has a significant shareholding in Octagon Developments Ltd who develop UK luxury homes. A recent award was for the best luxury home over £1 million.

Additionally Beechcroft plc, an upmarket retirement homes developer, was acquired in 2000. Developments are limited but will be of interest to retirees.

Both these sites can be accessed from the tool bar in Laing Homes.

Laing Homes generally has about thirty to forty active developments. Prices range from around £80,000 for a one-bedroom apartment to over £1 million for a luxury, detached house.

Laing Homes is accessible from the main site. Just click on the large **Laing Homes** icon. But it is also accessible from **www.laing-homes.co.uk**. The **Homes for Sale** button opens with an invitation to select a county.

The search results are presented with a small photograph, a location and a price. More detail can be requested. At this stage a full description is given of each type of house, including the floor plan. The location details include information on transport, shopping, sports, leisure, education and environment.

A site or development layout plan is also included. These are delivered by Adobe, which can be a bit slow. But when they do arrive they are beautifully presented.

The search results also extend an invitation for an **Etour**. This is impressive. It is quick to load and moves at a sensible pace. The tour can be stopped in any room. This is a stylish and effective tour. Floor plans are conveniently available with measurements in both metric and imperial.

There is a lot on this site, perhaps too much. Navigation on the site is not as simple as it should be.

A very good site, but don't get frustrated with the navigation!

www.westbury-homes.co.uk
Westbury Homes

Overall rating: ★ ★ ★ ★

Classification:	Builder	**Readability:**	★ ★ ★ ★
Updating:	Not Known	**Content:**	★ ★ ★
Navigation:	★ ★ ★ ★	**Speed:**	★ ★ ★ ★

UK

Westbury Homes claim to be one of the fastest growing providers of new homes in the UK. The company was formed in the early 1960s, and is currently one of the top six domestic house builders in the UK. Their current output is about 4,000 houses per year. They build from one to six bedroom houses in a variety of styles in over forty counties.

Homepage offers alternative routes to either Homefinder or Westbury plc. This latter site is a corporate site.

The **Online Homefinder** opens with selection by town or county. The search is quick and the property information is well displayed. Two more links are immediately available to either **Local Information** or to a more detailed examination of the properties through **Properties Available**.

Local Information is very thin, but a map is available. At any time in this process you can request a brochure, or contact Westbury direct through links on the top tool bar. A brochure request allows you to give further descriptions of what you are seeking, with a time scale for your move and a price.

Properties Available presents a small diagram of the house styles being presented on that particular development. Each type of property is named with a link to fine detail concerning the style. This includes elevation views and a floor plan.

At any time the searcher has access to the **Housestyles** button to obtain access to the full range of styles being developed by Westbury. The initial search is by number of bedrooms and then by the style. And one cannot fail to be impressed by the number of options available.

An attractive feature of the site is the 3D show home tour that is entered through the Homepage of Homefinder. The facility shows a range of properties ranging from two to six bedrooms. The tour is excellent and interactive.

This is an excellent site. It is a must for the new home seeker.

www.wilcon.co.uk
Wilson Connolly

Overall rating: ★ ★ ★ ★			
Classification:	Builder	**Readability:**	★ ★ ★ ★
Updating:	Not Known	**Content:**	★ ★ ★
Navigation:	★ ★ ★ ★ ★	**Speed:**	★ ★ ★ ★

UK

Wilcon Homes was formed in 1905. They were Major Housebuilder of the Year 2001. They are currently developing over 150 sites across the country. The company builds about 4,000 houses a year.

The **Homes for Sale** button immediately goes into **Home Search**. You can search by county or by development. The latter comes with a name only and there is no immediate indication of location. However a map location search is soon to be established on the site. This latter category also includes a development called **Coming soon**. This will keep the home searcher up-to-date with company developments.

The results are shown clearly and you merely move to the site of your choice. The types of properties that are on the site are shown. More details are obtained by clicking on the appropriate house style. The floor layout is revealed, together with full descriptions, including specifications. Measurements are in metric and imperial units.

They claim that they strive to make each home and development as varied and interesting as possible. Thus individual properties may vary from the illustrations.

SPECIAL FEATURES

The Local Community covers education, leisure, shopping and travel. A location map is included. This could have been more usefully included elsewhere. However the detail of most of the subjects is such that the new home seeker will have to refer to more authoritative local area sites elsewhere.

The 5% Deposit option states that on selected sites Wilcon Homes will pay the 5% deposit on condition that the mortgage is taken through their recommended advisors. This facility is not available on all sites and all houses.

The Part Exchange Scheme will allow you to quickly and conveniently sell your existing home but, as with the 5% option, this is only available on selected sites.

A well laid out and user-friendly site. It is a must.

Other Major House Builders

Redrow Group   www.redrow.co.uk
Crest Nicholson   www.nicholsonestates.co.uk
Bovis Homes   www.bovishomes.co.uk
Gleeson Homes   www.gleeson-homes.co.uk
Fairview New Homes   www.fairview.co.uk
Bewley Homes   www.bewley.co.uk

DIY Selling

Sites where property can be advertised for free vary enormously in quality. Additionally the list changes frequently. The internet sites connected to property are still in a formative stage and many will not become economically viable. Some will therefore simply amalgamate or disappear althogether. We have reviewed five of the best sites.

www.easier.com			
Easier			
Overall rating: ★ ★ ★ ★			
Classification:	Real Estate	**Readability:**	★★★★
Updating:	Regularly	**Content:**	★★★
Navigation:	★★★★	**Speed:**	★★★★
UK			

Easier may be described as a anti-estate agent site, with a mission to 'revolutionise the way homes are bought and sold'.

Easier facilitates private sales only and enables you to advertise your property on the Internet without charge. It claims to earn its keep from its business partners, drawn from providers of property-related services like conveyancers, valuers, insurers, mortgage providers, utilities and home maintenace firms who are prepared to pay for mass marketing rights.

Easier is divided into **Sell Your Home** and **Buy Your Home**. Registration is mandatory.

Sell Your Home enables you to list the details of your property, attach a description and photograph, modify the details and withdraw your property from the market. Property listing is rather comprehensive and should deter all but serious sellers.

Buy Your Home contains a search tool with filters by type of property, number of bedrooms, price range and garage/garden. You can search by postcode or map. Search results are sorted by newest listing, highest price first or lowest price first. You can store your search criteria for future use.

If you wish to make contact with a seller you should click on the **Send Your Details** button. The vendor's address is not disclosed. Your particulars are simply emailed to the vendor so that he/she will be able to contact you as soon as possible.

SPECIAL FEATURES

Easier chains For £100 (including VAT) you are provided with a weekly update of the progress of your transaction. Easier will contact each party in the chain and prompt them to hurry up. This service is currently on trial on a first come first served basis.

Easier messaging A free service where Easier acts as a neutral third party in collecting and forwarding offers, counter offers, acceptances and rejections. This service is also in pilot and is currently available on a first come first served basis.

Easier viewings You can bring in the the security company Group 4 to conduct a buyer's viewing session. The cost of a supervised tour of your property in your absence is a £60 + £35.25 p.m. + £23.50 per hour, and £23.50 + £17.65 p.m. + £23.50 per hour in your presence.

Easier pictures Easier will display one picture of the main property plus four pictures per additional room at no charge.

Easier 360-degree tour For £149 (including VAT) Easier will produce and display four rotating views of your home and one 360-degree view to be used as an email attachment to buyers.

Worth a look if you are interested in selling privately.

www.exchangeandmart.co.uk
Exchange & Mart

Overall rating: ★ ★ ★			
Classification:	Real Estate	**Readability:**	★ ★ ★ ★
Updating:	Weekly	**Content:**	★ ★
Navigation:	★ ★ ★ ★	**Speed:**	★ ★ ★

UK

The site database comes from *Exchange & Mart*, *Dalton's Weekly* and *Trade-It*. The site is simplicity itself – perhaps what one would expect of a magazine. After the opening page, a circular wheel gives access to all the opportunities presented by the magazine. **Property** has a section to itself.

The breakdown includes **Property for Sale, Property for Rent, Holiday Homes, Farms, Land & Small Holdings** and **Park Homes.**

Property for Sale is a simple list with no particular geographical orientation or style of property. Details come with a telephone number or an Email. There are over 400 properties available but it is its simplicity that makes the visit worthwhile. The list can be scanned quickly, but the quality and the nature of the information varies significantly.

Holiday Homes & Timeshare showed a wide geographical distribution ranging from America to Cyprus.

Most of the **Property for Rent** comes in the form of single rooms with a wide geographical distribution.

A limited site, but has quick access to hundreds of properties.

www.homefreehome.co.uk
Homefreehome

Overall rating: ★ ★ ★ ★			
Classification:	Real Estate	**Readability:**	★ ★ ★ ★
Updating:	Not Known	**Content:**	★ ★ ★ ★
Navigation:	★ ★ ★ ★	**Speed:**	★ ★ ★ ★

UK

The site tells us that the private individual can buy or sell a house with absolutely no fees, no commissions and no agency charges. Registration is required, more for security reasons than anything else, but it is free, quick and simple.

The aim of the site is to make housing transactions totally transparent and to remove the stress when a third party with a financial interest becomes involved. The site is financially maintained by selected banner advertising within the site.

The **Buying site** immediately puts you into property selection. You can enter price in bands of £50,000, the type of property and the area or town. You are presented with a selection of properties with the opportunity to ask for further property details. Descriptions are very full and some properties come with photographs. If you are interested you can send the seller either your name and email address or your telephone number.

The **Selling site** has two entry points. You can either enter new details or amend existing details. You need to have full details of your property available as the information required is comprehensive. In addition to property details, other information such as council tax and condition of the property can be entered.

Drop-down boxes give you an adequate choice and significantly help the process. Each room can be described in detail, and there is the opportunity to add any further information that you consider appropriate. This includes local area facts and features.

Up to four photographs can be displayed with the property.

The **Just Looking** site is for unregistered browsers who wish to view the preliminary details of houses inside the **Buying** site. But properties cannot be viewed in detail.

The site uses four strategic partners for mortgages, legal matters, financial services and removals. The site claims that discounts have been negotiated with these partners.

The site is well organised. This is the place to give your property the full, descriptive treatment!

www.loot.com
Loot

Overall rating: ★ ★ ★

Classification:	Real Estate	Readability:	★★★★
Updating:	Daily	Content:	★★
Navigation:	★★★★	Speed:	★★★

UK

The company was launched in 1985 as the UK's first free ad-paper. Loot advertises itself as the biggest A to Z of classified ads with over 300,000 advertisements in 400 classifications. It can contain about 2,000 property advertisements.

The site is completely free, even if a photograph is included. The advertisement is kept for 14 days. Contact is by Email and Loot automatically provides a link when it appears online.

The top tool-bar shows the main sites in the property section.

The **Search** button brings up the main search menu, and here you can enter the type of property, the type of advertisement you wish to search and price range. Location can be entered either by postcode or region.

The results are very basic and very similar to the printed edition. There is an opportunity to go for more information but this is a bit thin. A site map is available. The age of the advertisement is also given.

Coverage across the country is sparse and the majority of properties appeared to be in the major conurbations, particularly London. Properties are concentrated towards the bottom half of the market.

Place a free ad requires simple, free registration.

The site mirrors the printed edition. It is easy to follow, and certainly worth a visit.

www.purehomes.com
Pure Homes

Overall rating: ★ ★ ★ ★			
Classification:	Real Estate	**Readability:**	★ ★ ★ ★
Updating:	Daily	**Content:**	★ ★ ★
Navigation:	★ ★ ★ ★	**Speed:**	★ ★ ★ ★

UK

Revenue for the site is achieved by advertising revenue from businesses that operate in the property services sector and who advertise on the site. The Homepage is well laid out and leads immediately to some recommended specialists. There is an **estate agent,** a **financial planner** and a **builder.**

The main property guide starts at **UK Property for Sale.** This brings up a comprehensive list of counties and other significant areas in the UK. This is well laid out and easy to read. Clicking on the relevant area brings up a simple screen where your only selection parameter is a price range. The ranges are up to £75K, from £75K to £150K, from £150K to £300K and finally over £300K.

This is the only selection parameter, but it works surprisingly well. Photographs are available with some properties. Contact Emails or telephone numbers are given.

The **Overseas Property** button produces a list of some 15 countries or places. These include the USA and Australia. The treatment is similar to the UK properties.

A site that concentrates on the essentials, it is what you want when searching for property; but, the coverage is of concern.

DIY Selling Paid Advertisement Directory

Sites where the individual can advertise his own property, like the free sites, vary enornously in quality. Additionally, it is clear that the management behind the site varies significantly.

The introduction has already outlined some of the drawbacks to the private sites. For the purchaser it is worth bearing in mind that the vendor has most to gain from this arrangement. This is not to say that there are not some good properties here, but some of the usual market constraints may not necessarily be present. We have reviewed four of the best fee-paying sites for you.

www.housenet.co.uk
Housenet

Overall rating: ★ ★ ★

Classification:	Real Estate	**Readability:**	★ ★ ★
Updating:	Daily	**Content:**	★ ★ ★
Navigation:	★ ★ ★ ★	**Speed:**	★ ★ ★ ★

UK

The site is operated by Ryland Technology Ltd. It is a non-profit making site and is used to advertise their expertise as web developers. The site was set up in 1996.

Anyone wishing to advertise property can enter an advert directly into the database. The user is given a password. This can then be used to amend details.

Adverts are deleted automatically nine months from the date of last amendment.

The site has a free listing for text adverts for residential property for sale in the UK and Ireland. A photograph can be added to the basic text advert for £17.63

But full details including a photograph can be submitted by mail and the details and photograph will be scanned onto the site. The cost is £29.95 (inc VAT) for a six- month period.

There are some 2,500 properties on the site. About 92% come from private advertisers and 8% per cent from estate agents. In addition, it is possible to view the selection of estate agents.

The Homepage immediately leads into a search for property. The initial area for search is a huge tract of country. This then reveals the second details screen. This screen allows a much tighter designation of area, the type of property, the number of bedrooms and a price range. The search results are a simple list of properties with location, type, bedrooms and price. Local area maps are available and contact is by Email or telephone.

Search requests are completed quickly. Details that have not been modified for six months are automatically deleted.

The **Mortgage** site links to a firm of mortgage and financial advisors. There is some good information on the first page. There is a very good summary of good mortgage buys. This is useful to get you tuned into what the market has to offer.

The site also contains a **mortgage calculator** that completes a simple payment schedule for both repayment and interest only mortgages. There is also a facility to apply for **mortgages on-line**.

The **conveyancing** site has some links to other similar sites. But the major attraction is an online quotation for conveyancing, whether buying or selling. It gives an excellent summary of the costs involved.

The **buyers** button lets you register your details with Housenet. You can then receive Email updates of suitable properties.

The **sellers** button shows the screen for advertising your property and giving property descriptions. You can also modify previous information.

The **Environment** check leads into local area programmes. **Areacheck.co.uk** is reviewed in chapter four.

Home insurance offers a number of links to brokers.

This is a well-designed site that has a good mix of information. Property coverage may be a bit thin, but it is well worth a visit.

www.houseweb.co.uk
HouseWeb

Overall rating: ★ ★ ★ ★			
Classification:	Property	**Readability:**	★ ★ ★ ★
Updating:	Regularly	**Content:**	★ ★ ★ ★
Navigation:	★ ★ ★ ★	**Speed:**	★ ★ ★ ★

UK

HouseWeb is the doyen of online real estate in the UK with a lineage extending all the way to 1996 and with 150,000 properties on the books. It is primarily a non-agency site but it does carry links to estate agents and can search across agency sites if it cannot find a compatible property in its own database.

* You can advertise your main residence, and holiday home for sale, rent or exchange (including holiday homes).

* Read the selling, buying, mortgage, insurance, moving and exchanging and professionals generic guides.

* Obtain life assurance quotes from within the Houseweb Service Centre (see below) and general insurance quotes from Screentrade (**www.screentrade.co.uk**).

* A Web Directory links you to panels of utilities providers, insurance services, mortgage services, solicitors and conveyancers, relocation agents, removal firms, van/car hire rental companies and a shopping channel currently comprising QXL (**www.qxl.com**) the online auctioneer and BarclaySquare.

* Review a selection of best buy mortgages (fixed rate – with or without redemption penalties, variable, variable discounted, capped and first time variable; and house prices) and mortgage quotes from MortgageShop, E-Loan, CharcolOnline and FredFinds.com.

Houseweb Service Centre is a unique innovation that claims to be the first ever online quotation service for homeownership-related goods and services, where the participating suppliers are selected by recommendation rather than by dint of having paid to be represented on the site.

Consumers can request quotations for homeownership-related goods and services required. For example, if you are moving house the system will generate a maximum of three quotations from removal firms operating in your postal area who are expected to contact you within 48 hours. When you use this service for the first time your personal details are captured so that you never have to enter them again.

Suppliers are vetted initially by Houseweb, but are subsequently rated by consumers who have used their services. The long-term result is that the panel of suppliers is effectively selected by personal recommendation. Remarkable!

A useful site which is well worth a visit.

www.mondial-property.co.uk
Mondial Property

Overall rating: ★ ★ ★

Classification:	Real Estate	**Readability:**	★ ★ ★
Updating:	Daily	**Content:**	★ ★
Navigation:	★ ★ ★ ★	**Speed:**	★ ★ ★ ★

UK

This is a very simple site with a range of clear, uncluttered screens. The site was formed in April 1999 with the aim of providing a shop window for property owners wishing to advertise and sell their homes privately without the services of an estate agent.

The site is interactive in that it enables the seller to create his own advertisement on screen using the site pro-forma description page. The result is that the full property details with photograph is very similar to the details produced by estate agents.

The site has nearly 800 properties and is frequently visited by expatriates. It is receiving between 12,000 and 15,000 visits per week.

The main **Buying** screen allows the input of county, type of property, minimum number of bedrooms and a price range. This allows inputs in £50,000 bands up to £200,000.

The search results are shown in tabulated form. A key button allows a request for more details of the property you are interested in. Further searches are easily activated with the further search button.

www.thegoodwebguide.co.uk **65**

The **Selling** screen gives the option to either register a property for sale or to update an existing property. The terms and conditions for these transactions are clearly shown. The advertisement will stay on the site for 6 months, after which time it will be removed unless you give instructions to the contrary. You may change the selling price any number of times you wish.

There is an advertising fee of £35 including VAT.

The form for passing property details to the site is very comprehensive. This leads to more than adequate property descriptions. Once entered it is possible to see a preview of the advertisement.

The site is worth a visit whether buying or selling.

www.propertybroker.co.uk
Propertybroker

Overall rating: ★ ★ ★ ★

Classification: Real Estate		**Readability:**	★ ★ ★
Updating: Daily		**Content:**	★ ★ ★ ★
Navigation: ★ ★ ★ ★		**Speed:**	★ ★ ★

UK

The site was founded in March 1998. This is a service for both sellers and buyers. The site aims to be the most successful way to buy and sell property in the London and M25 area.

The cost of using the site is £97. There is no commission to pay when you sell. Details are sent to the site by Email using a Registration Form. Property Broker arranges to take free digital photographs of the property and erect a free For Sale board. Exposure of the property is maximised by advertising in the *Evening Standard* and the *Mail on Sunday*.

If on a visit to the site you cannot find the property you want a notification form can be completed. Thereafter you will receive an Email each time a match to your requirements is added to the site.

The Homepage offers routes for buyers, sellers and for a mortgage service.

The **Buyers** button leads to simple and advanced searches.

The **Simple Search** is for those who have seen a for sale board. Only the road or street name is required.

The **Advanced Search** allows preferred location, postcode and description to be added. This includes price range and the number of bedrooms. The search results are displayed in price order with a minimum of information. However, more information can be requested and good quality information and photographs are available.

From the Homepage you can access the **Sellers** link. Property details can be entered on-line, sent by Email or transmitted via conventional telephone. Property Broker will take the photographs, and erect a for sale board. This service applies to the London and M25 area.

This is a professional site and is well worth a visit.

Renting and Letting Property

It is clear that many property sites on the net are trying to be all things to all men. Some of the big sites carry out every function we can see within the property market. This includes renting and letting. Below are two information sites and some of the sites which either specialise in this form of activity or which have been previously reviewed and which seem to be doing a good job.

INFORMATION SITES

ARLA
www.arla.co.uk

The Association of Residential Letting Agents has over 1,200 member offices located throughout the UK. On their website their search functions allow a search by ARLA agent, a search by district or town, a search by county and a search by London area or Borough.

The information for landlords is excellent. It has been specifically designed to aid landlords who are looking to let their property through a residential letting agency and consists of questions that every landlord should ask and the answer they should receive.

RENTAL/LETTING SITES

www.accommodation.com	The Accommodation Directory.
www.asserta.co.uk	Reviewed under property websites.
www.citylets.co.uk	Letting in Scotland.
www.findaproperty.com	Reviewed under property websites.
www.fish4homes.co.uk	Reviewed under property websites.
www.letsdirect.co.uk	Property to rent across the UK.
www.lettingweb.com	Rental in Scotland.
www.londonhomenet.com	Properties in London.
www.londonproperties.co.uk	Good portal site.
www.net-lettings.co.uk	London. Agents and area rent guide.
www.primelocation.co.uk	Reviewed under property websites.
www.propertyservices london.co.uk	Greater London.
www.rightmove.co.uk	Reviewed under property websites.

Chapter 03

check out the local area

What makes the perfect house?

Certainly the answer cannot be given without reference to the local area, the environment and the local facilities. Indeed, it may be that in some consumer's eyes the house itself is not necessarily the most important factor in this significant financial transaction.

What is certainly true is that when we are satisfied with local area, the environment and the local facilities then, and only then, can we really be happy about the house. The development of the Internet has given to consumers an invaluable facility. We can now look at the quality of life a new location will bring. Consumers are now able to look at quality of life, just as much as at the quality of the brickwork!

As with the property, a visit to the local area is still essential. But certainly with the sort of information you can find here, you will be one step ahead.

In this chapter we give you the best sites available to check out the local area. You can then judge for yourself whether this is the best location to satisfy your full requirements.

General Sites

There are some very good general sites that cover a large number of features.

Up My Street
www.upmystreet.co.uk

This is the mother and father of all local websites and as such warrants its own web site description. This is found at the end of the chapter.

Areacheck
www.areacheck.co.uk

By making use of an Area Check report, the company claims that you will be fully aware of the key factors that are important to your family in the forthcoming move. The report covers some 15 subjects, and these include noise pollution, traffic, environmental issues, crime and police activity and schools.

The site states that research is carried out over a seven-day period. Fees within the UK average out at around £250 for a week's surveillance. You are provided with a full report of the findings.

At a fraction of the price of an average house in UK today, the prospective buyer may feel that this is money well spent. It will certainly prevent the new purchaser making a very expensive mistake.

Location

There is no doubt that to be able to locate your new house properly is a huge bonus. There is much that can be gained from the perusal of a local map.

Multimap
www.multimap.com

The site can find any address in the United Kingdom. The search is quick and efficient. It is invaluable in assessing the local area. There are other facilities on the site. Driving directions within mainland Great Britain are available and for those with some distance to travel there is help in locating a hotel.

Streetmap
www.streetmap.co.uk

This site offers similar facilities in address searching and street map facilities. The search can be carried out by street, postcode, place or Ordnance Survey grid reference. Searches are performed quickly, and there is little else on the site to get in the way of a quick, clean search.

Environment

This is a subject that is bound to increase in importance. And it is better to find out the drawbacks now before you move in. Additionally it would be madness to allow someone else to discover the potential environmental faults with your location when you start your own selling process. Adverse environmental reports at this stage could significantly affect your wealth, or even your ability to sell.

Homecheck
www.homecheck.co.uk

This is a remarkable site. The site states that it is the ultimate free guide to flooding, subsidence, pollution, landfill sites, schools, property prices and crime rates in the neighbourhood.

The homebuyer merely has to type in the postcode and you will immediately be presented with a map and reports covering many aspects of your area. In addition to those already mentioned, radon, coal mining, landslip, landfill waste, historical land use, air quality and pollution are all covered.

Each category comes with a useful coloured bar chart, and each topic comes with a further information button.

Additionally it is possible to Email the report to your lawyer for their initial comment. Or you can request that they purchase a Homecheck Professional Report on your behalf.

A detailed and site-specific report is available for only £29.38 including VAT.

There are additional information channels on the site. This is a site that the new purchaser must visit.

Home-envirosearch
www.home-envirosearch.com

This is an extremely comprehensive search site and includes ten areas of potential contamination. In addition to those we have heard about it also covers transmitters and radioactivity. The search is completed quite simply by the insertion of the postcode and the report appears immediately.

But the homebuyer should be aware that this is a report on neighbourhood risks and is not a property-specific search. The homebuyer should ask his solicitor to obtain a property-specific Home-envirosearch report.

The report costs £39 including VAT and is available through the post within 48 hours from receipt of order.

A further report from Plansearch Residential is available through this site and this provides essential planning and floodplain information to homebuyers. The report is available within 48 hours from receipt of order.

www.thegoodwebguide.co.uk 71

Schools

Office for Standards in Education
www.ofsted.gov.uk

This is a focused website for parents who wish to look at inspection reports. OFSTED's remit is to improve standards in education through regular independent inspection, public reporting and informed independent advice.

The site is well laid out with a very professional feel to it. It is easy to follow. The Inspection Reports section covers some 14 main areas. The links to each area provide further details of the inspection work and access to the inspection reports themselves. Searching for an individual school is quick and simple. With this facility so readily available, every parent can take a realistic view of schools in the area of their new home.

Scotland
www.hmie.gov.uk

This is equivalent to the OFSTED site in Scotland. There is a very professional feel to the site and access to school reports could hardly be more simple. This is a site parents in Scotland must visit.

Northern Ireland
www.deni.gov.uk

This is the education site for Northern Ireland. There is certainly more on the site in terms of information. Access to Inspection Reports is quick and easy. And a useful feature is a School Location Map.

Independent Schools Information Service
www.isis.org.uk

This is the official website for the 1,300 UK schools accredited by the Independent Schools Council. The site is provided and maintained by the Independent Schools Council Information Service.

The search for independent schools can be by school name, keyword, postcode or county. The search is comprehensive and quick.

Independent Schools of the British Isles
www.isbi.com

The site for the Independent Schools of the British Isles includes 3,200 independent and fee-paying schools and residential special needs schools in the British Isles. It also features summer schools and revision and retake courses.

The search facility for schools is impressive. A general search covers features such as day, boarding, boy, girl, scholarship and fees. Further searches include location, school facilities and special needs.

The information on the site is current as schools are allowed to update their details in January and July each year. For those considering the independent sector the site is certainly worth a visit.

The Scottish Council of Independent Schools
www.scis.org.uk

The Scottish Council of Independent Schools (SCIS) represents around 96% of pupils in the independent sector in Scotland. Although SCIS cannot recommend specific schools to parents, general advice is given about the choice available, about different types of school and about the facilities for special needs.

The website contains comprehensive details of all Scottish schools represented by the SCIS. You can search for a school by specific categories and by location. There are about ten different categories of school shown, ranging from Senior Schools, through all the combinations of age and sex, and conclude with specialist schools. About 22 locations within Scotland are available for selection.

The General Information section covers a wide range of factors of specific interest to parents considering the independent system in Scotland.

Department for Education and Skills
www.dfes.gov.uk/parents

This is a government-sponsored site and tells you about your child's education and how you can help. The website is designed to help parents, carers and guardians find out more about their children's education, health and welfare.

The Find section of the site allows you to find information on any subject quickly and easily.

Site Search lets you type in details such as maths or science information. Site Index lists every piece of information on the site in alphabetical order.

Possibly the most valuable to parents who are in the process of moving is the 'Multiple Search' facility. This allows you to search school performance tables, school websites and OFSTED school reports at the same time. The search is carried out either by postcode or school name. This is a comprehensive facility and one which most caring parents will want to use.

www.thegoodwebguide.co.uk 73

Medical Services

National Health Service
www.nhs.uk

This is the official gateway to National Health Service Organisations on the Internet. It provides national information about the NHS and also connects you to your local NHS services.

The Local Services search, accessed from the Homepage, provides a complete and searchable directory of dental practises, GP surgeries, opticians, pharmacies and NHS organisations.

The services are easily accessed either by the facility required or the postcode. The nearest five services are quickly displayed, together with full details. A map is available, if required.

Access to the NHS in Scotland, Wales and Northern Ireland is from the Homepage. This is an excellent site and invaluable for people thinking of moving.

Surgery Door
www.surgerydoor.co.uk

This is an exceptionally good site for everyone and not only those people in the process of moving. There is a huge amount of both general and specific medical information on the site. There is information on over 400 medical conditions, as well as diets, medications and procedures.

And the database is continuously being updated to provide both the latest and most up-to-date information.

There is a complete section allocated to the NHS, including access to local services. The section also includes information on Benefits and Entitlements and Support groups. The site is informative and interesting, and well worth a visit.

Public Transport
www.pti.org.uk

This site will enable you to determine just how easy it will be to travel to and from your new location.

The site claims to cover all travel by rail, air, coach, bus, ferry, metro and tram within the UK. This includes the Channel Islands, Isle of Man and Northern Ireland. It also includes rail, ferry and coach travel between the UK and mainland Europe.

Such is the mass of information available that this is not an easy site to use. But the Homepage has a button ' How to use this site'. This is invaluable. However, the amount of information is overwhelming. Fortunately there are telephone hotlines for those who get lost!

But for the family who are considering a move, or who maybe considering a more rural type of life, an examination of transport alternatives will be invaluable.

www.upmystreet.co.uk
Up My Street

Overall rating: ★ ★ ★ ★ ★			
Classification:	Local Area Guide	**Readability:**	★ ★ ★ ★ ★
Updating:	Not Known	**Reliability:**	★ ★ ★ ★
Navigation:	★ ★ ★ ★ ★	**Speed:**	★ ★ ★ ★ ★

UK

UpMyStreet claims to be the real-life guide to the neighbourhood. On the Homepage is one of the invaluable helpmates we always wished for but didn't know where to find. It is the **Postcode Finder**! Just add the details and up pops that postcode.

The site covers local services, property prices, schools, the Council's record and offers classified advertisements.

On entering either town or postcode a local map is presented. This can be manipulated in almost any manner. It is excellent in helping the home seeker locate very precisely a particular property.

Property Prices shows the average price of property types within the area, and compares them with the average in England and Wales. However it is clear that such figures add little to local knowledge as it is the close location detail of the property that counts. A graph is produced that compares local price trends over the last six years with the national average. This is a useful tool.

The **Find My Nearest** site is, so they claim, the quickest and smartest way to track down the businesses and services nearest to your house. Nine major categories are listed including education, health, restaurants and hotels. There is also the ability to search for categories such as tradesman. This is a comprehensive facility. Under Education alone there are nearly 40 different categories.

The main source for all listings is from **Thomson Directories**. **What's On** covers a wide range of entertainment including cinemas, theatres, pubs and restaurants. And the results cover not only the immediate area, but the surrounding area as well.

The **ACORN** profile is a classification system indicating broad lifestyle trends in the area. Whilst certainly comprehensive, it did not add anything that could not more usefully be completed with eyes and ears.

Council Performance produces some very useful statistics. It will confirm if the dustmen are efficient, and whether much re-cycling goes on. It gives statistics on the library, social services, public transport and so on. And certainly it can act as confirmation of what you yourself see in the area.

Education figures are produced down to individual schools, but the figures on **Policing and Crime** are a bit thin.

This site is a must before you buy – miss it at your peril.

Chapter 04

selecting the right mortgage

The UK has a diverse and accessible market in mortgages. There is a wide range of providers and products. Currently in the market there are well over 100 different mortgage lenders offering over 3,000 products.

It is not surprising that the wealth of information available confuses the consumer. It is not possible to keep up to date just by reading magazines. Not only is this time consuming but also because of the lead-time in printing, they are often out of date before the reader sets eyes upon them.

In this chapter we outline the best sites available to you for both conventional and specialist mortgages.

The building societies are the traditional mortgage lenders and number about 60. In many cases they have more than 100 years of experience. The societies are mutual organisations and as such do not have shareholders.

The mutual building societies should be able to offer more competitive mortgages than the banks because building societies do not have to pay dividends to shareholders. Dividend payouts can be up to half of a bank's profit and are typically worth 0.5% to 0.75% of interest rate benefit.

The high street banks have been mainstream lenders for more than 20 years. They are easily accessible and provide competitively priced mortgages. Around half-a-dozen of the big building societies have become banks in recent years, but they remain major mortgage lenders.

Insurance companies have been in the market for some time. Some insurance companies have linked up with banks that are active mortgage lenders.

The specialists are often referred to as centralised lenders since they have no branch network. They work from a central office, and now more frequently over the Internet. Most specialist lenders offer mortgages for non-standard borrowers, such as the self-employed, part-time workers and those with poor credit records.

If you want a mortgage from a traditional lender with plenty of experience, then a building society is a good option. You will not go far wrong with a large national building society. The high street banks score highly on convenience as they have a large high street presence. The specialist lenders often have attractive interest rates and where specialist lending may be the only option.

Most homebuyers want to buy a mortgage from someone who has access to all lenders. Yet paradoxically nearly half still go to banks or building societies selling their own products.

A face-to-face meeting remains by far the dominant mortgage sales channel. There is a clear desire to have human contact when arranging a mortgage. An across-the-table meeting gives the consumer the opportunity to receive a full explanation of products and to ask detailed questions. Consumers want advisors who demonstrate independence and depth of knowledge and competence.

Consumers use the Internet to complete their homework before entering into meetings with any form of advisor or broker. It is simply a question of obtaining the maximum benefit from the meeting and obtaining the best possible mortgage.

Currently few consumers arrange their mortgage on line, even though over 20% of mortgage lenders could accept an application via the Internet. But programmes will become increasingly user-friendly and cheaper costs will be passed on to the consumer. For the lenders, transactions over the Internet are five times cheaper than the telephone and ten times cheaper than a high street branch network.

Certainly finding a mortgage through an online broker is more convenient than trawling through lender's websites. And many broker sites provide a link to the lenders site where an online application form may be provided.

One thing that makes the better sites stand out is the opportunity to speak to a real life advisor over the telephone if things go wrong. Most sites have a telephone call facility, but unless you have a separate telephone line for the Internet you may have to turn off your connection in order to take the call.

But as mortgage sites improve more and more of us will apply online.

The future will not go away.

Directories of Mortgage Brokers

It makes sense to convince yourself that you have completed a thorough search of the mortgage market before committing to the large financial outlay that is involved in house purchase. The sources of finance are bewildering in their number and sometimes in their complexity.

In the following pages we have reviewed eight broker sites from which you will certainly be presented with the best arrangements on the market today.

For those borrowers who have developed, or wish to develop, a brand loyalty, we have included a list of lenders websites. Over 100 of them. Good hunting!

Find
www.find.co.uk/mortgages/mrpc

This is the independent gateway to all UK financial websites. The site has a very comprehensive list of mortgage brokers that can be accessed from the Mortgage and Loan centre.

Finance Link
www.financelink.co.uk

A comprehensive list of mortgage brokers and lenders is available by clicking on the Mortgage Broker link on the Homepage. There are well over 100 brokers displayed.

The Best Mortgage Broker Websites

www.adviceonline.co.uk			
Advice On Line			
Overall rating: ★ ★ ★ ★			
Classification:	Intermediary	**Readability:**	★ ★ ★ ★
Updating:	Daily	**Reliability:**	★ ★ ★ ★
Navigation:	★ ★ ★ ★	**Speed:**	★ ★ ★ ★
UK			

Advice On Line are UK Independent Advisors directly regulated by the Personal Investment Authority. They are not linked to a product provider. They offer advice via an associated company called Park Row Associates plc. This company has a team of 180 advisors working around the country.

The site has an excellent mortgage advice centre. It is clear, comprehensive and, above all, it is useable. The Homepage has boxes for advice, obtaining quotes, borrowing money and so on. Within the box **Request Advice** there is a subheading **Mortgages**. This leads to the **Mortgage Advice Centre**. This has ten subsections, the majority of which are relevant to a mortgage search.

The second section opens with a section devoted to **See the Savings available by Re-mortgaging**. This is a simple table that allows you to see at a glance the savings to be made by switching to a more competitive mortgage. Feed in your current interest rate, payment method, loan outstanding,

78 www.thegoodwebguide.co.uk

property valuation and term remaining and the answer is produced. Click on **Rate Beaters** and a list of those lenders who can improve on your current mortgage is shown. The mortgage listings are shown in descending order of savings per month. This is an excellent mortgage tool.

The **Top Ten by mortgage type** section of the advice centre is just that. By opening a simple screen, with one click the top ten mortgages in that category are shown. The results are shown with mortgage lender, rates, loan to value and other factors depending on the type of mortgage being searched.

It is possible to **Search the entire UK mortgage market** by means of a quick search. While some of the fields are mandatory, the form is easy to complete and the search is quick. It is certainly a useful tool to narrow the field and thus make the market that much more manageable.

For an overview of the market click on **Browse the Complete UK mortgage tables**. Indeed it may be useful to complete the use of this tool before going on to use other options.

This overview of the market can be supplemented by viewing the full **List of UK lenders plus rate history**. Over 100 lenders are shown, together with their interest rate history.

The final tool is a **Mortgage Payments Calculator**. This requires only four parameters. They are loan amount, term, interest rate and the interest calculation method.

This is a simple yet excellent site. It contains almost everything required in the mortgage search.

www.blays.co.uk
Blays

Overall rating: ★ ★ ★ ★

Classification:	Intermediary	Readability:	★ ★ ★ ★
Updating:	Daily	Reliability:	★ ★ ★
Navigation:	★ ★ ★ ★ ★	Speed:	★ ★ ★ ★

UK

Originally Blays provided financial information to national papers, banks, building societies and financial institutions. The main homepage outlines quite clearly what services the site offers. One area is devoted entirely to mortgages.

On the welcome page to Blays Mortgage Services there is the option to select the type of mortgage you wish to examine. Their mortgage section contains variable, fixed, discount, capped, first-time buyers, buy-to-let and re-mortgage.

After selecting the type of mortgage, the next page is a brief description of the mortgage characteristics and an indication of the number of tables that are going to be shown. While this figure can often be quite high, the programme handles this well. It isn't possible to get lost or confused.

Most tables show a list of the major lenders and the searcher can go to an all-lenders table if appropriate. Each table shows the minimum and maximum loan figures, the charge rate, the fee, the base rate and compulsory insurance. A tool bar across the top reminds the searcher of the mortgage options.

This simple site is brilliant. Although there are no mortgage wizards, calculators etc., the site is one that must be visited.

www.charcolonline.co.uk
Charcol Online

Overall rating: ★ ★ ★			
Classification:	Intermediary	**Readability:**	★ ★ ★
Updating:	Regularly	**Reliability:**	★ ★ ★
Navigation:	★ ★	**Speed:**	★ ★

UK

Charcol is a leading independent mortgage advisor and IFA. CharcolOnline displays and transacts in variable, discounted, fixed and capped rate, tracker, buy-to-let, self-certified, impaired credit, flexible and 100% mortgages.

There are a series of Mortgage Wizards for First Time Buyers, Home Purchase, Remortgage and Buy-to-Let. They are similar but specialised wizards will dwell on relevant areas and lead to different parts of the market. The Wizards will note income, property and credit history details so that the mortgage shortlist will show relevant products.

For first time buyers try the new **What-Sort-of-Mortgage-Suits-Me Calculator**. A series of eight questions gently identifies your earning and interest expectations, your likely outgoings and your predilection for accelerated capital repayment. The programme produces a chart that identifies mortgage types that are likely to be most suitable. The first time buyer can then return to the Wizard and search for the cream of the recommended mortgage categories.

Search The Wizard produces a table of suitable schemes for which you are likely to qualify, displayed by lender, type, description, APR, offer term, redemption details and compulsory insurances, in ascending order of APR. You can view details of specific offers in the View Details column.

The table can be resorted in ascending order of monthly payments (years 1, 2 and 3), total cost over 3, 5 and 7 years and redemption costs over years 2, 3 and 5. You can also compare the search results against the products of one nominated lender, and you can apply online by clicking on the **Apply Now** button adjacent to any listed mortgage offer.

OTHER FEATURES

Rapid Remortgage Wizard For a selection of mortgage products with no requirement for valuation or legal fees, agreement in three days and the funds within two weeks.

Overseas Mortgages & Advice via Conti Financial Services with expertise in 15 countries.

CredoRealty Deposit Guarantee is a facility for deferring the deposit on exchange; allegedly cheaper than bridging loans.

Best Buys on the Homepage displaying the best fixed rate, capped and discounted mortgage products by lender, rate (and APR), offer term and redemption penalty.

Guides to homebuying, mortgages, remortgages and buy-to-let.

This is a good site with an efficient search engine. Recently acquired by Bradford and Bingley, this is a mortgage site worth a visit.

www.eloan.co.uk
E-LOAN Ltd

Overall rating: ★ ★ ★ ★ ★			
Classification:	Intermediary	**Readability:**	★ ★ ★ ★
Updating:	Regularly	**Reliability:**	★ ★ ★ ★
Navigation:	★ ★ ★ ★ ★	**Speed:**	★ ★ ★ ★

UK

E-LOAN Ltd is the Uk mortgage arm of E-LOAN, Inc, a provider of information on mortgages, credit cards and small business loans.

This E-LOAN number enables potential borrowers to choose a mortgage (or a car loan) that suits their circumstances, and to initiate applications online.

The site purports to be 'totally independent' and provides access to about 1,700 prodcuts from some 50 mortgage lenders.

SPECIAL FEATURES

Buy a Home The most direct route through the mortgage search for knowledgeable borrowers. In addition to entering income, loan-to-value and property details, you are asked to select your preferred types of repayment or interest-only mortgages from Variable Rate (Standard and/or discounted and term), Fixed Rate, Special (capped, cashback), Flexible, Current Account and Integrated Banking.

You can also specify your tolerance for early redemption penalties and overhang.

Remortgage A similar procedure to Buy a Home.

Help me find the right mortgage A wizard to help you find the right type of mortgage. A series of questions about earnings, loan to value, the attraction of low and level payments in the early years and the likelihood of accelerated capital repayments leads to a recommendation as to the most appropriate types of mortgages.

The search engine produces a series of tables of ten offers for each recommended or selected loan category, itemised by monthly payments, payable rate, standard rate, APR, lenders fee, cashback, mandatory insurance, redemption fee period and flexible features.

Search results are displayed in ascending order of monthly payment, payable rate, APR, standard rate, cashback or customer fees. Click on the name of the product to view the mortgage terms, rate and payment forecast over ten years and estimated completion costs for any loan listed. Finally, check the 'tick to compare' box adjacent to any two offers to compare by terms, mortgage payment, mortgage interest and early redemption penalty over any period up to ten years.

Click on the apply button adjacent to your chosen mortgage to commence the online application. This part is a bit of a slog, but the programme really means business and you are going to have to provide these details anyway.

Submit your application online and wait for an E-LOAN consultant to contact you.

www.thegoodwebguide.co.uk **81**

OTHER FEATURES

There is a special section devoted to Flexible Mortgages that allow accelerated or reduced capital repayments, cashbacks, payment holidays, calculation of interest on a daily basis and no early redemption penalties. Each feature has its own calculator showing the effect of utilising that facility on the remaining term of the mortgage or the level of future repayments.

This section also explains current account and integrated banking mortgages (sweepers) and contains an excellent calculator that demonstrates how sweeper accounts can save you money by offsetting your credit balances against your most expensive forms of debt first.

Mortgage Questions explains the various types of mortgages (fixed, variable, capped, current account, discounted, integrated banking and flexible).

There is a selection of guides on the home buying and remortgaging process, mortgage purchase strategies, loan-to-value considerations, debt consolidations, flexible mortgages and APR.

A class act. The search engine allows the sorting of the results table by multiple criteria. The layout is clean and trim and the site is decidedly nippy. The only reservation is the relatively small number of affiliated lenders.

www.ftyourmoney.co.uk
Ftyourmoney

Overall rating: ★★★

Classification:	Newspaper	**Readability:**	★★★
Updating:	Daily	**Reliability:**	★★★★
Navigation:	★★★	**Speed:**	★★★

UK

The *Financial Times* must be the doyen of financial newspapers. There is a significant section on **Mortgages and Homes**, but it is primarily a mortgage section.

The section is substantial and larger than a number of specialist mortgage sites.

The top button on the left hand list is **Compare and Buy-Mortgages**. This leads immediately to a **Mortgage Wizard**. This leads through a series of standard questions concerning mortgages. Each question itself has a question mark next to it. If the question is not understood, a click on the question mark brings up an explanation.

The wizard is somewhat long and ponderous and may not be what most searchers want at the early stage of a search.

After completing the detail, a wide variety of lenders and types of mortgage are presented. The results are presented with all the detail that could possibly be required.

Further amendments can be made to the search particulars with a minimum of fuss. Comparison is easier if you choose one type of mortgage at a time.

The **Refine Search** button at the bottom of the results page allows a number of filters to be put into the search parameters. These include features such as insurance, fees and redemption penalties.

The Homepage also leads to a substantial Learn centre. This is useful browse material. The **Find the Right Mortgage** section has a useful summary of the main types of mortgage. For those uncertain about mortgages and mortgage terminology, some time spent browsing this section will pay dividends.

The **Tools** section is useful to check the financial viability of the project. **Mortgage Affordability** gives a calculation of your potential mortgage payments and is a must.

Mortgage Tables, accessed from the left hand tool bar, presents an excellent array of mortgage options that can be examined by simply selecting from a table.

The site has a lot to offer, but you have to work for the benefits. It is excellent for the experienced house mover.

www.marketplace.co.uk
Bradford & Bingley

Overall rating: ★ ★ ★ ★			
Classification:	Intermediary	**Readability:**	★ ★ ★
Updating:	Daily	**Reliability:**	★ ★ ★ ★
Navigation:	★ ★ ★ ★	**Speed:**	★ ★ ★ ★

UK

Bradford and Bingley are independent advisors and offer a full range of financial products. We have reviewed the site under estate agents but it has a very strong mortgage section and has therefore been included here.

The site offers hundreds of products from more than 30 of the UK's major lenders. Additionally they offer exclusive mortgage deals, negotiated directly with lenders, specifically for their own customers.

No broker fees are charged if the mortgage is purchased online. A full support team is available merely by clicking the **Call me** button.

The **Mortgage** button leads to a range of options including first time buyers, home purchase, remortgage and buy to let mortgages.

Before you look at the mortgages on offer, a visit to the **Calculators** may be opportune. The site has a choice of four calculators. **How much will it cost** offers a rough idea of what your monthly payments would be for a given loan amount and interest rate. **How much can I borrow** gives you a feel for how much you may be able to borrow. The **Flexible**

www.thegoodwebguide.co.uk **83**

Mortgage Calculator allows you to assess the sort of savings available should you use the overpayment facility of a current account mortgage

Finally on offer in the Calculator section is **What sort of mortgage suits me**. A number of simple screens allows you to assess your current and future position. The results are produced as a series of simple horizontal graph lines showing the degree to which each particular mortgage suits your profile. It certainly takes some of the mystery out of the process. Perhaps this should have come first.

An additional useful feature comes from the **Help** button. This runs into the **Frequently asked Questions** site. This site needs time and care to handle. But it offers one of the best series of questions and answers available on the property-related internet.

From the main **Find a Mortgage** page there is immediate access into the **Mortgage Wizards**. The wizards themselves are easy and quick to complete. Many of the questions appear with an answer already programmed in. This is an excellent feature for those less sure of handling a mortgage questionnaire. There is a facility to apply online or to view further details.

As with so much that Bradford & Bingley do, this site is of high quality and well worth a visit.

www.moneyextra.com
MoneyeXtra Mortgages

Overall rating: ★ ★ ★

Classification:	Intermediary	Readability:	★ ★ ★ ★
Updating:	Regularly	Reliability:	★ ★ ★ ★
Navigation:	★ ★ ★ ★	Speed:	★ ★ ★ ★

UK

This site carries details of 2,000 mortgage products from 120 lenders, of which about 320 can be transacted online. You can use this site to search for variable, fixed, capped and discounted variable rate, flexible, cashback, buy-to-let, self-certified, impaired credit history and euro mortgages.

You can confine your search to mortgages that can be transacted online or extend it to all mortgages on site. The initial questionnaire follows the pattern of other sites. Search results are displayed in tabular form, in ascending order of the payable rate. Other column headings are period for payable rate, standard variable rate, cashback and redemption penalties/conditional assurances. The table is not sortable by any of the column headings.

You can click on the provider's name to study the fine print of the mortgage deal and a handy calculator works out your monthly payments.

Application is initiated by clicking on the Apply button adjacent to each table entry.

A good range of mortgages to browse but the lack of a sortable results table lets this site down.

www.moneynet.co.uk
Moneynet

Overall rating: ★ ★ ★ ★			
Classification:	Intermediary	**Readability:**	★ ★ ★ ★
Updating:	Daily	**Reliability:**	★ ★ ★ ★
Navigation:	★ ★ ★ ★	**Speed:**	★ ★ ★ ★

UK

Moneynet is an independent service that aims to provide comprehensive information on the UK personal financial market. They claim not to operate from a restricted panel of providers. Because they make no charge for the inclusion of product information you can be certain you are getting an overview of the market as a whole.

The Homepage has a large number of sections with one section devoted entirely to a wide range of mortgages.

The **Residential mortgage** section claims to show thousands of products from over 100 lenders. Information is updated daily. The mortgage search itself is sophisticated. The search results can be displayed in three useful ways. They can be displayed showing the lowest headline rate, by the total cost of each product and the largest cash back. This facility is one of the best on the internet and will be invaluable in helping you to make the most of your money.

By clicking the **Residential Mortgages Search** a simple questionnaire is brought up. It requires basic information only. But the search can be refined by including or excluding options on insurance, redemption penalties, restricted geography and whether products come only via brokers.

This is an excellent search function.

The **Flexible Lifestyle** window offers exactly the same basic information screen and simply presents a different range of mortgages.

All the remaining windows offer similar facilities. But in particular the **Remortgage Calculator** within the **Remortgage** section is excellent. But you will need to have done your homework first. Full information is required on your current mortgage to enable you to complete the questionnaire. There is a link that takes you to more detailed information on how to interpret the results.

The **Arrears, CCJs and Non-status** section allows those with a less-than-perfect credit history to search out the best loan. The search facility is swift and again allows the results to be displayed by headline interest, total cost and cash back.

The mortgage section on this site is first class. Those seeking a mortgage must make a visit to the site.

www.thegoodwebguide.co.uk **85**

www.moneysupermarket.com
Money Supermarket

Overall rating: ★ ★ ★

Classification:	Intermediary	**Readability:**	★ ★ ★ ★
Updating:	Regularly	**Reliability:**	★ ★ ★ ★
Navigation:	★ ★ ★ ★	**Speed:**	★ ★ ★ ★

UK

Money Supermarket is primarily a search tool for seeking out and transacting in the most competitive mortgages, personal loans, credit cards, cash ISAs and savings accounts. There are also helpful calculators for finding the best electricity, gas, telephones and mobile deals.

The service is the creation of Mortgage 2000, a leading provider of online mortgage and loan comparison software to Independent Financial Advisers.

The site specialises in fixed, capped and discounted rate, flexible and cashback mortgages for a wide variety of applications; from home purchase to remortgaging, self build, equity release for the elderly, Right-to-Buy and capital raising for home improvements, debt consolidation, school fees, holidays and cars, second properties, divorce and business purposes.

The preliminary questionnaire has up to eight steps. The depth of the interrogation depends on the purpose of the loan, your employment status, whether or not you can produce three years accounts (for self employed and company directors) and credit history.

You can build your results table from any of capped, fixed or discounted rate mortgages. Variable rate mortgages are only included if their initial payments come in below the capped or discounted rate products.

The final table lists available mortgages in ascending order of true cost (total cost including arrangement and valuation fees less cashbacks, and interest and capital payments) over a selected period. The other column headings are mortgage type, initial rate, duration of offer term, base rate, monthly payment and cashback.

The table is not sortable but the search can be refined further by restricting the mortgage offers in the table to cashback and/or flexible, no redemption penalties and no overhang (like no redemption period after the fixed/capped/discount term has finished).

Clicking on the **details** button reveals the fine print. In some cases you can apply online by clicking on a red, flashing **How do I apply?** button. This takes you through to an online application form that you eventually email off to the provider of your choice. Alternatively you can order a hard copy application form.

This is a workmanlike site that offers a good mortgage section. It is worth a visit, but it is easy to get distracted.

www.mortgageseekers.co.uk
Independent Association of Estate Agents

Overall rating: ★ ★ ★ ★ ★

Classification:	Public Service	Readability:	★ ★ ★ ★ ★
Updating:	Daily	Reliability:	★ ★ ★ ★ ★
Navigation:	★ ★ ★ ★ ★	Speed:	★ ★ ★ ★

UK

The Independent Association of Estate Agents provides this site as a free service to the general public. They are a non-profit making organisation dedicated to maintaining high ethical and professional standards in estate agency. All lenders in the UK are given facilities to show their full product range and services. The service is completely free.

The **Find a Mortgage** button leads to **A Few Notes About Using The System**. This is worth an examination. Alternatively you can go straight to **Take Me To The Mortgages**. This is the heart of the site.

The **Mortgage Wizard** searches the market for products that match your requirements and calculates package costs for each product selected. This wizard is simple and easy to use. The selection of mortgage type for comparison is well laid-out. The results are presented in a clear way. The Wizard does not frustrate the searcher at all. It is an absolute bonus.

The **Quicksearch** is excellent. By inputting a minimum of detail, it is possible to obtain very quickly an overview of the UK mortgage market. Indeed, to make the most of the Mortgage Wizard, it is probably better if you first narrow down your search by using Quicksearch.

The **Quick Calculator** calculates the monthly mortgage payments for interest only and repayment mortgages.

The **Rate Beater** is simply that. First feed in the most basic details of your current mortgage, including your current interest rate, payment method, outstanding loan, value of property and term remaining. Immediately you are presented with a list of lenders who can beat your current mortgage. This is a very thought-provoking screen and a must for the cost-conscious homeowner.

The **Maximum Borrowing** facility is standard, but an excellent feature is that it allows you to separate out each individual lender.

The **Mortgage Tables** lists mortgage products by classification and provides general product information. This is another excellent feature because with a single click you can list all the lenders offering products in your desired category.

Top Mortgages is based on the lowest rate in each category without an early redemption penalty or a stepped rate.

The **Apply on Line** button is easily found at the top of the page. There is a facility to select any suitable lender, including inserting your own lender if you wish. The form is simple to complete. Based on the information submitted, it allows a lender to indicate a willingness to lend in principal.

This is an excellent site. Miss it at your peril. Use it and you will save hours – and perhaps also pounds!

www.yourmortgage.co.uk
Your Mortgage

Overall rating: ★ ★ ★ ★

Classification:	Magazine	Readability:	★ ★ ★ ★ ★
Updating:	Daily	Reliability:	★ ★ ★ ★ ★
Navigation:	★ ★ ★ ★ ★	Speed:	★ ★ ★ ★ ★

UK

Your Mortgage magazine is an independent consumer finance title published monthly since 1986. From the outset the site is user friendly and easy to follow.

The **Find a Mortgage** button on the top tool bar leads to four options. These are **Find a Mortgage, Mortgage Wizard, Search all Mortgages** and **Latest Mortgage Deals**.

Find a Mortgage offers help, particularly for the first time buyer. There is a section on the buying process. But for those who know exactly what kind of mortgage they are looking for, you can search the latest mortgages by mortgage type, duration and lender.

If you want to avoid looking through hundreds of different mortgages you should move direct to the **Mortgage Wizard**. This will search all the mortgage products for you and quickly narrow the choice. It can also be used to initiate contacts with lenders. It requires the answer to only three questions before presenting a list of suitable mortgages.

Search all Mortgages is quick and easy to use. Mortgages are listed in ascending interest rate order. Some lenders have restrictions, and fuller details can be requested.

Your Mortgage can contact any of the lenders listed to arrange for them to contact you. This is a very fast facility and is one of the best on the internet.

Most of the mortgage products are listed in **Find a Mortgage**. But the site regularly reviews a selection of the latest mortgage deals and the results are shown in **Latest Mortgage Deals**.

The **Property Price Predictor** calculates very rapidly what your house will be worth in five years time. If you can provide an accurate price post-1996, you will be able to obtain a more accurate prediction.

Calculators is located on the top tool bar and is an excellent field. The **Mortgage Comparison Calculator** allows you to compare four different loan profiles ranking them by monthly payments. The tool is simple to use, the graphics are excellent and the figures easy to manipulate. The **Flexible Mortgage Calculator** allows you to plan how to get the most from a flexible mortgage. It shows quite simply how over- and under-payment and payment breaks will affect your repayment schedules. It requires hands-on experience, but it is an invaluable tool. The **Mortgage Repayment Calculator** is a simple tool computing loan repayments and total interest payable over the long term.

The site also offers information on a wide range of specialist mortgages.

This site should not be missed. It offers exactly what the mortgage seeker needs. Five well-deserved stars.

Specialist Mortgages

Many of the broker websites will give access to specialist mortgages. It is common sense that if your circumstances are such that you feel that you need a specialist mortgage, then why not go to a specialist lender. They are more likely to understand your personal circumstances and you will be more likely to obtain your mortgage.

Kensington Mortgage Company provide home loans to borrowers who cannot be helped by the traditional High Street and direct lenders. The company was established in 1995 to provide home loans to people who effectively did not fit the mould. Some 25% of people who apply for a mortgage do not come within the criteria required of the mainstream lenders.

They now claim to be the UK's largest non-conforming lender. Initially the products were only available through mortgage intermediaries, but now the public can apply through the website or by the telephone.

In the **Our Promise** section the company promises to examine every application on its merits. The product range covers almost all adverse credit and unusual income or employment situations.

The **Mortgage Enquiry** section contains a **Product Wizard** that is interactive. There is no requirement to give name and address to access the product information. The only information required relates to your loan requirements, your employment circumstances and any credit problems you may have incurred.

The **Wizard** will identify the mortgage products available based on the information you supply. It enables you to select which of them most suit your requirements. It will also display a detailed illustration. This can then be sent to you with an application form. You enter just as much or as little information as you feel appropriate. The results are comprehensive in that they can be displayed in seven different ways. This includes by rate, net monthly payments and loan to value.

Product Overview is an excellent presentation of the products available. It is well laid out and simple to use.

The **Frequently Asked Questions** (FAQ) field is comprehensive and should be the first port of call for many visitors to the site.

This site is well worth a visit by anyone having the slightest problems in obtaining a mortgage.

www.platformhomeloans.com
Platform Home Loans

Overall rating: ★ ★ ★			
Classification:	Non-conforming lender	**Readability:**	★★
Updating:	Daily	**Reliability:**	★★★★
Navigation:	★★★	**Speed:**	★★★

UK

Platform Home Loans is part of the Britannia Group of Companies. Britannia Building Society, which is the second largest in the UK, acquired the company in February 2001.

They are a mortgage lender with specialist lending criteria. This allows them to lend to individuals with a less-than-perfect credit history. They confirm that such a condition now applies to one person in four who applies for a mortgage.

They launched into the UK market in 1997. Such has been their success that they have received a string of awards. These include Best Non-Standard Mortgage Lender for three continuous years from 1999 to 2001.

The principle behind the operation is that an individual's past is not necessarily a good indication of their future ability to pay a loan. In short they look at an individual's ability to pay rather than simply relying on credit scoring systems.

The **Product Portfolio** is a comprehensive list of the full range of products available. There is a huge amount of information there.

The **Standard** product is ideal for clients with all levels of arrears and CCJs. The **Light Adverse** is ideal for clients who fall in between the traditional high street lender and their successful non-conforming range. Their **Fast-track** product is suitable for clients who do not wish to provide references. The **Right-to-Buy** is ideal for clients wishing to buy their council property.

Whilst the information is easy to access and comprehensive, it is not always easy to handle. This facet of the site is weak.

Products from the company can only be accessed via an Intermediary. An **Introducer** can obtain a **Decision in Principle**. He simply completes the form on the screen and sends it to the company.

There is a lot in this site. It is certainly worth a visit.

www.ucbhomeloans.co.uk
Nationwide

Overall rating: ★ ★ ★ ★

Classification:	Specialist lender	**Readability:**	★ ★ ★ ★ ★
Updating:	Not Known	**Reliability:**	★ ★ ★ ★
Navigation:	★ ★ ★ ★ ★	**Speed:**	★ ★ ★ ★

UK

UCB Homeloans is the specialist mortgage lender of Nationwide Building Society. They have over 15 years experience in providing self-certification mortgages. They provide mortgages for individuals who cannot prove their income in the traditional way. These people would probably be self-employed, contractors or company directors.

As self-employed people they may not be able to produce audited accounts. Or they may be employed but their payslips vary because they are paid commission or bonuses as well as their basic salary.

The **Products and Rates** section offers a well laid-out screen with 4 main mortgage options. These are flexiplus, discount, fixed rate and buy-to-let.

Product Information is on the same screen. This gives access to useful information on all self-certification mortgages. Information is presented on repayment methods, fees and charges, insurance and payment difficulties. This is certainly worth a visit as it is well laid out and easy to assimilate. The mortgage information is equally well presented and the obvious questions have been more than adequately answered.

The self-certification mortgage scheme provides borrowers with a real opportunity to take advantage of the equity locked in their home. Similarly it provides an ideal refinancing opportunity for many. These include the self-employed, contract worker or other employed worker who would benefit from a self-certification mortgage where they don't have to prove income.

The **Toolkit** site also has a borrowing calculator, a mortgage calculator, a house price calculator and a budget planner. All are simple, efficient and easy to use. The mortgage calculator calculates for both interest only and repayment loans.

The **Insurance** site offers a mortgage payment protection product and home insurance.

For buyers who wish to take the process further there is a **Contact Us** button that gives details of telephone, fax, Email and postal address. For those who wish to move things along faster, there is a **Call Me** button.

The **Information Request** allows you to submit personal and mortgage details.

This is an excellent site for anyone who may not be able to prove income. The site is impressive.

www.paragon-mortgages.co.uk
Paragon Mortgages

Overall rating: ★ ★ ★ ★

Classification:	Specialist lender	Readability:	★★★★
Updating:	Daily	Reliability:	★★★★
Navigation:	★★★★★	Speed:	★★★★

UK

Paragon Mortgages are Buy-to-Let specialist mortgage lenders. The **Mortgage Wizard** takes you quickly and efficiently through the **Buy-to-Let** questionnaire. They offer a number of profiles. These include Portfolio for the professional landlord, Company Let, and Non-portfolio for landlords who obtain their main income from separate employment and who may wish to buy one or two extra properties. There are only nine very simple questions to answer before you receive the information you require.

Tools and Calculators has five sections.

House Evaluator will estimate a house value for you using Regional Price Indicators. But, as the site admits, this is only a generalisation and true prices depend on a whole range of other factors including local conditions.

The **Savings Calculator** allows you to use your own growth predictions to calculate the savings necessary to repay an interest only mortgage. This is swift and efficient.

The **Income Calculator** will work out the minimum income required to support a given loan.

The **Buy-to-Let** calculator is absolutely essential for anyone entering this particular market. The calculator will tell you whether you should borrow over a five-year period to enter this market. This is an invaluable aide for those new to the market.

Finally in this section the site offers some free **Spreadsheets** that cover some ten separate areas. Once familiar with these there is very little reason for buy-to-let projects to go wrong.

The **Reference Area** contains the key **Product Details**. They are presented individually with a comprehensive description for each product. This can be difficult to take in.

There is a facility to **Apply Online** to obtain an **Agreement in Principle**.

This is an excellent site for buy-to-let landlords and for those about to enter the market.

www.renovationmortgages.co.uk
Ecology Building Society

Overall rating: ★ ★ ★			
Classification:	Specialist lender	**Readability:**	★★★★
Updating:	Not Known	**Reliability:**	★★
Navigation:	★★★★	**Speed:**	★★★★

UK

This is the website of the Ecology Building Society which is based in West Yorkshire. It is a mutual building society founded in 1981. Money deposited by savers is used to grant mortgages on properties and projects that help the environment.

Savings placed with the Society fund mortgage lending on energy efficient housing, ecological renovation, derelict and dilapidated properties, small-scale and ecological enterprise and low-impact lifestyles.

It is clearly stated that to ensure those applying for membership of the Society share their environmental and ecological concerns they will be asked if they are members of a green organization before they will accept a savings account. But you do not have to be green to get an ecology mortgage.

The **Mortgage Interest Rate** screen shows all their current rates for residential, commercial and but-to-let properties. Some conditions are attached to the mortgages and these are clearly explained. Some discounts are available.

Monthly payment calculators are also shown.

The **Enquiries** page allows for the passage of personal and mortgage details together with details of the mortgage you are interested in.

This site is small, neat and simple and invaluable if you want an ecology mortgage.

Websites for other Specialist Mortgage Lenders

Self-build can be both satisfying and financially rewarding. But it requires good planning, attention to detail and staying power.

An overseas mortgage may contain all the dangers associated with changing exchange rates. Bridging loans whilst most certainly solving an immediate problem, always pose exit problems of a very dangerous kind. If any of the associated arrangements fall through, your finances may suffer disastrous consequences.

Self-Build for the Self-employed
www.buildstore.co.uk

Overseas Mortgage Specialists
www.astute-mortgages.co.uk
www.expatnetwork.co.uk
www.expatsite.com
www.moneynet.co.uk
www.mortgagesoverseas.com

Bridging Loans
www.acceptances.co.uk
www.directloan.uk.net
www.lerwick.plc.uk
www.moneypointfinance.co.uk

Major Lenders

Borrowers may develop a loyalty to a particular lender. There is always an advantage in this that the borrower can build up a track record with one single institution. For those who wish to examine the product range from one particular lender in detail, the following is the list of the major UK lenders.

Abbey National	www.abbeynational.co.uk
Alliance & Leicester	www.alliance-leicester.co.uk
Allied Irish Bank	www.aib.ie/gb
Bank of Ireland	www.boi-mortgages.co.uk
Bank of Scotland	www.bankofscotland.co.uk
Barclays Bank	www.barclays.co.uk
Barnsley Building Society	www.barnsley-bs.co.uk
Bath Investment Building Society	www.bibs.co.uk
Beverley Building Society	www.beverleybs.co.uk
Birmingham Midshires	www.askbm.co.uk
Bradford & Bingley	www.marketplace.co.uk
Bristol & West	www.bristol-west.co.uk
Britannia Building Society	www.britannia.co.uk
Cambridge Building Society	www.cambridge-building-society.co.uk
Capital Home Loans	www.chlmortgages.co.uk
Century Building Society	www.century-building-society.co.uk
Chelsea Building Society	www.thechelsea.co.uk
Cheltenham & Gloucester plc	www.cheltglos.co.uk
Chesham Building Society	www.cheshambsoc.co.uk
Cheshire Building Society	www.thecheshire.co.uk

Chorley & District Building Society	www.chorleybs.co.uk
Clydesdale Bank plc	www.cbonline.co.uk
Coventry Building Society	www.coventrybuilding society.co.uk
Cumberland Building Society	www.cumberland.co.uk
Darlington Building Society	www.darlington.co.uk
Derbyshire Building Society	www.thederbyshire.co.uk
Direct Line Financial Services	www.directline.com
Dudley Building Society	www.dudleybuilding society.co.uk
Dunfermline Building Society	www.dunfermline-bs.co.uk
Earl Shilton Building Society	www.esbs.co.uk
Ecology Building Society	www.ecology.co.uk
Egg	www.egg.com
First Direct	www.firstdirect.com
First National	www.firstnat.co.uk/ mortgages
Mortgage Company	
First Trust Bank	www.firsttrustbank.co.uk
Furness Building Society	www.furnessbs.co.uk
Future Mortgages	www.future-mortgages. co.uk
Gainsborough Building Society	www.gainsboroughbs. co.uk
Halifax Mortgages Direct	www.halifax.co.uk
Hanley Economic Building Society	www.thehanley.co.uk
Harpenden Building Society	www.harpendenbs.co.uk
Hinkley & Rugby Building Society	www.hrbs.co.uk
Holmsdale Building Society	www.holmesdale.org.uk

Household Mortgage Corporation	www.hmcplc.co.uk
HSBC	www.hsbc.co.uk
Igroup	www.igroup.co.uk
Ilkeston Property Services	www.ipbs.co.uk
Intelligent Finance	www.if.com
Ipswich Building Society	www.ipswich-bs.co.uk
Irish Permanent	www.ipmortgages.co.uk
Kensington Mortgage Company	www.kmc.co.uk
Kent Reliance Building Society	www.krbs.co.uk
Lambeth Building Society	www.lambeth.co.uk
Leeds & Holbeck	www.leeds-holbeck.co.uk
Leek United	www.leek-united.co.uk
Legal & General	www.landg.com
Loughborough Building Society	www.theloughborough. co.uk
Manchester Building Society	www.themanchester.co.uk
Mansfield Building Society	www.mansfieldbs.co.uk
Market Harborough Building Society	www.mhbs.co.uk
Marsden Building Society	www.marsden.co.uk
Melton Mowbray Building Society	www.mmbs.co.uk
Mercantile Building Society	www.mercantile-bs.co.uk
Monmouthshire Building Society	www.monbsoc.co.uk
Mortgage Express	www.mortgage-express. co.uk
National Counties Building Society	www.ncbs.co.uk
Nationwide Building Society	www.nationwide.co.uk
Natwest Mortgage Services	www.natwest.co.uk

www.thegoodwebguide.co.uk 95

New World	www.mynewworld.com	Sun Bank Plc	www.sunbank.com
Newbury Building Society	www.newbury.co.uk	Swansea Building Society	www.swansea/bs.co.uk
Newcastle Building Society	www.newcastle.co.uk	The Co-perative Bank	www.co-operativebank.co.uk
Northern Bank	www.nbonline.co.uk		
Northern Rock	www.northernrock.com	The Teachers Building Society	www.teachersbs.co.uk
Norwich & Peterborough Building Society	www.npbs.co.uk	Tipton & Cosely Building Society	www.tipton-cosely.co.uk
Nottingham Building Society	www.thenottingham.com	UCB Home Loans	www.ucbhomeloans.co.uk
Portman Building Society	www.portman.co.uk	Ulster Bank	www.ulsterbank.com
Preferred Building Society	www.preferredmortgages.com	Universal Building Society	www.universal.uk.com
		Virgin One Account	www.virginone.com
Principality Building Society	www.principality.co.uk	Weslyan Financial Services	www.wesleyan.co.uk
Progressive Building Society	www.theprogressive.com	West Bromwich Building Society	www.woolwich.co.uk
Prudential Banking	www.pru.co.uk		
Royal Bank of Scotland	www.rbos.co.uk	Yellow Brick Road Direct Mortgages	www.yellowbrickroad.co.uk
Saffron Walden Building Society	www.swhebs.co.uk	Yorkshire Bank	www.ybonline.co.uk
Sainsbury's Bank	www.sainsburysbank.co.uk	Yorkshire Building Society	www.ybs.co.uk
Scarborough Building Society	www.scarborough.co.uk		
Scottish Building Society	www.scottishbldgsoc.co.uk		
Scottish Widows Building Society	www.scottishwidows.co.uk		
Shepshed Building Society	www.theshepshed.co.uk		
Skipton Building Society	www.skipton.co.uk		
South Pacific Mortgages Ltd	www.spml.co.uk		
Staffordshire Building Society	www.staffordshirebuildingsociety.co.uk		
Standard Life Bank	www.standardlifebank.com		
Stratford Railway Building Society	www.srbs.co.uk		
Stroud & Swindon Building Society	www.stroundandswindon.co.uk		

Chapter 05

need help to move?

Moving, as we are repeatedly told, is one of the most stressful events we encounter. Any help that is available to reduce that stress has to be welcome. What we are not told is whether it is the property search itself that is stressful or the whole range of associated activities.

Perhaps some casual thoughts on the problem will soon identify that the house search can bring some pleasures in its own right and it is, in fact, when the perfect place has been found that the nightmares truly begin. Packing up and moving, with all the necessary legal matters, paperwork and general hassle is enough to turn anyone

away from even starting the new property search in the first place.

Most property sites themselves offer a range of services. Many sites simply use the ones we are reviewing here. But it is easy to get lost and to lose focus.

There is a wealth of help available on the net. Indeed, so much is available that it is stressful just searching out the good sites! But we have selected the best sites for you. Follow these sites through and you will arrive at the perfect house with the minimum of stress.

General Planning

www.ukonline.gov.uk

This is a government site and is one of the most comprehensive advice sites on the web. Get into search mode and type in 'moving home', and everything will be there for you. It is possible to change to any one of the four home countries. Advice is available through a number of categories from thinking about the move to planning, searching and making the move.

The breadth of subjects should satisfy absolutely everyone. Benefits, childcare, legal, transport services, schools, medical, planning etc.; it's all there.

This site is all very well laid out and well worth a visit.

www.reallymoving.com

The site contains an absolute mass of information dealing with the moving process. Some of the major activities such as buying a property and mortgage selection are produced by other companies which we have reviewed elsewhere. In particular the property section is powered by Property Finder and the mortgage section is powered by CreditWeb. Local information comes from UpMySreet.

Online quotes are obtainable from solicitors, surveyors and removal, insurance and cleaning companies. This is obtained by filling in one simple form. The quotes come from a network of professionals and companies across the UK. Importantly the site states that there is no mark-up on the price you would otherwise be quoted if you telephoned direct. It is claimed that most quotes are displayed on screen instantly, while others are Emailed within a few hours.

For those who want real organisation there is a Planning and Reminder guide. It presents some good checklists that could be of use to most people and will certainly make that move go all the more smoothly.

The Tell Everyone One You Have Moved facility is a free service. Your details only have to be entered once. From there the companies and organisations you want to know about your address change are informed.

This is a useful site, particularly for those moving for the first time. But there is something there for everyone who wants to take some of the pain out of moving.

www.themovechannel.com

This is a directory site and as such is a jumping off point to many other sites on the net. The site has also been shown under property directories. For those moving home the site offers much useful information. But for information on the process of moving itself, click on 'Moving House', which can be found under Site Finder.

Moving House has eight separate sections. These include local area information, conveyancing, surveyors, removals and storage, self-hire vans, travel and transport, relocation and utilities.

There is a mass of helpful information here. This is a good site; however, you will really have to devote a lot of time to it.

ADVICE ON MOVING

www.goodmigrations.co.uk

The site claims to be the home-moving expert. Certainly it is comprehensive and everything is there for the home-mover.

'Get Organised' gives an insight into the 25 things you must do when moving home, including what you do when and in what order. But you do have to register with the site before you can gain access to the information.

House movers may well be aware of most of the planning steps, although using the site will certainly bring some organisation to your move.

For those who wish to conduct their move through the Internet, this site is ideal. You are electronically directed to the professional services one needs to move, and you can task them from your armchair.

This site is certainly comprehensive. Indeed, it is a very advanced site and helps remove some of the pain from the moving process. It is definitively worth a visit.

MOVING DETAILS

www.ihavemoved.com

The site offers the house-mover the ability to change address with service providers, utility companies, TV licence authorities, government agencies, financial institutions, magazines and loyalty cards.

The site claims that the simple 3-step process only takes about 15 minutes. House-movers may consider this preferable to writing numerous letters or simply waiting an eternity whilst holding a telephone listening to queue music.

The service is free. The company tells that they make their money by partnerships with the UK's leading companies and by advertising and promotions on the site.

The site is worth a visit. It can make life much easier, and that has to be welcome.

REMOVALS

www.barmovers.com

This is the site of the British Association of Removers. The BAR has represented the professional moving industry for over 100 years. It is not surprising that they recommend anyone moving should choose a BAR member.

Over 1,500 companies world-wide are available through the site. The search is very simple and very quick. The 'Choose your Remover' can be activated on entering a postcode and selecting the service required. A list of suitable companies is then provided.

If you like those providing a service to be represented by a professional body, and to adhere to a code of conduct, this simple and effective site may give you the answer.

www.roarsreport.co.uk

This is the site for The National Register Of Approved Removers and Storers. ROARS will enable those moving home to identify with certainty a removal company capable of safely undertaking their work.

ROARS employs industry experts to act as inspectors. They visit companies annually to see if they meet ROARS accreditation criteria. Accredited removers will send a copy of a ROARS report with every quotation they offer the public.

LEGAL

The number of legal sites on the web is legion, and a significant number of property sites offer links direct to solicitors.

www.lawsociety.org.uk

The Law Society is the professional body for solicitors in England and Wales. This is a large and complex site. But home movers may wish to visit 'Solicitors Online', which is accessed from the Homepage. This will enable you to search Law Society records to find law firms or even individual solicitors. The searches are simple and quick.

Also of potential interest is the section on Legal Specialities. Unfortunately for those who require a conveyancing service, most of the law firms seem to 'specialise' in this area. Perhaps that is why the public generally feel unhappy about the quality of service they receive when moving home.

www.legaladvicefree.co.uk

This is an excellent website, particularly for those with legal questions. Indeed, it could be said that for the laymen it is the parent of all legal websites. Within our sphere of interest it covers House Buying, House Selling, Household Insurance, Landlord and Tenant, and Neighbour Disputes.

The relevant section will bring up a comprehensive series of questions and answers. Certainly all the obvious questions have been both asked and skilfully answered. However should you have a question hitherto unanswered, you can simply Email the site and you will receive an answer.

The questions are laid out in a perfectly logical sequence, and you can find your way quite clearly through the house buying process.

The site also has a list of solicitors throughout the United Kingdom.

This site is primarily an information site. But it is invaluable to anyone involved in property. And it is certainly worth a visit before you go to see your solicitor!

www.easier2move.co.uk

The site claims to be the easiest way to instruct a solicitor when buying, selling or re-mortgaging your home.

For layout, and clarity of information, it is difficult to fault this site. And on the point that really matters, the site guarantees that the price you are quoted for the conveyancing is the price you will pay. Additionally, if the sale falls through there is no fee. And this applies if the transaction does not go ahead for any reason whatsoever.

The online conveyancing quotations are excellent. They are well itemised, clear and easy to understand. Similarly the online case reports for all types of transactions are excellent. Subsequently it is very easy to track the progress of your case.

For those who do not wish to move from the comfort of their own armchair, this must be the way to run a property transaction. The site is even worth a visit just to see how a good, single-purpose site should be laid out.

www.onlineconveyancing.co.uk

This site offers a very similar conveyancing package and the terms look competitive. It is possible to track your mortgage at any time throughout the year. The tracking information is clear and complete.

The site is virtually dedicated to conveyancing and benefits enormously due to the simplicity that this allows. There is a free, no obligation 'Quick Quote' service which will allow the bargain hunter to quickly compare notes. This is a site certainly worth a visit.

CONFLICT RESOLUTION

Before contacting a solicitor, it may be prudent to approach one of the ombudsmen who may be able to help.

The Ombudsman for Estate Agents
www.oea.co.uk

The OEA scheme is devised to address disputes between Member Agencies and individuals acting in their private capacities. An individual with a complaint against a Member Agency must first exhaust the internal complaints procedure of that Member Agency concerned. The website shows that over 4,000 offices are members of the scheme.

The Financial Ombudsman
www.finacial-ombudsman.org.uk

The Financial Ombudsman Service has the power to award up to £100,000 in damages to an aggrieved policyholder. Using an insurer that is part of the Ombudsman scheme offers better consumer protection.

The Office of Supervision of Solicitors

Of course it may be your solicitor you are unhappy with. If so go to The Office of Supervision of Solicitors. This can be found under the Law Society website. In particular they investigate complaints about the quality of solictors' service and the standard of professional conduct.

SURVEYORS

www.rics.org.uk

This is the official website of the Royal Institute of Chartered Surveyors. This is the world's leading professional body addressing all aspects of land, property and construction.

From the Homepage, the 'Find a Surveyor' tab is the immediate point of interest. If you are looking for a surveyor in a particular location, merely click the 'Location' tab.

Additionally, should there be some particular features about your property on which you require a specific report, there is a 'Specialisations' tab showing surveyors with specific skills. There are over 100 different specialisations listed.

For those who want an authoritative survey report from a member of a professional body of high repute, this is the site to visit.

www.surveyline.com

This is a national network of over 200 UK Chartered Surveyors who offer a complete range of property advice. Whilst most lenders will require a valuation by one of their panel surveyors for their own purposes, there are situations when you may wish to commission your own Valuation Report. Cash purchase, matrimonial disputes and probate are situations where this may apply.

The advantage of this site, particularly for the cost conscious, is that you can request a quote.

www.cwsurveyors.co.uk

Countrywide surveyors are the largest residential survey business in the UK and operate from 140 locations. They are appointed valuers to virtually all the major UK lenders.

The site offers the residential homebuyer a full range of services ranging from a mortgage valuation report or homebuyer surveys to energy surveys. The office locator is quick and simple to use. Simply select a county and press 'Go'. A list of towns and cities covering the chosen county will appear. Office details can then be accessed.

This is a very effective site. For the consumer in a hurry, this may be the site to investigate and avoid any fuss.

Chapter 06

all about the house

If moving is one of the most stressful of occupations, then finding the right tradesman must be a large contributory factor to that stress. Tales of the bad builder and the bad tradesman are legion. Indeed, television programmes are now made showing the completion of totally botched jobs.

But there are some well-proven rules for seeking out the reliable builder or tradesman.

The first is selection by recommendation. Self-evidently if you can take a recommendation from a relative or friend who has used a reputable builder, or even better, has had a similar job completed by him, then that is the route to go.

If you are moving to a new area, this method may not work. But by the judicious use of the trade sites we have listed, local consumer groups, use of local knowledge from the estate agents themselves and firms of managing agents, you should be able to keep out the cowboys.

Cowboys are always 'working in your area' offering special discounts or contactable only by mobile telephone.

When you do have a list of creditable names, it is worth asking more than one firm to quote for the work. You should also make sure they quote from the same schedule of work that you yourself have produced. To compare different builders' quotes from their own written estimates is notoriously difficult.

The production of the quote itself is a good indicator of professionalism. How has it been presented? How long did it take? Can you understand it? How long is the job forecast to last? Does it include everything, including raw material, in the quote? Answers to these questions will certainly prevent you from accepting a poor quote. In short, is it professional? And do you have confidence in it?

In the following pages is a list of some sites in which you can have confidence.

BUILDERS

www.fmb.org.uk

This is the website of The Federation of Master Builders. They state that they are the leading voice for all medium and small-sized building companies in the UK. The Federation states quite clearly that the FMB promotes professionalism and high quality workmanship throughout UK. Only those builders and specialists who can prove their skills and good business standing are accepted as members of FMB.

The most important tab is the Find a Builder tab. There are some 12,500 members on the FMB database. The site is quick and simple. Simply select a category and a location and search

Also, the site contains some good general information for use by the public. It is worth a visit. For those who cannot obtain a recommendation for a good, reliable builder, this site is a must.

TRADESMEN

www.registeredplumber.com

The Institute of Plumbers lists some 3,500 members in their Members Directory. A local plumber can be found merely by entering a postcode. All the members listed have had to prove their plumbing competence through recognised qualifications or extensive experience. The site can also be accessed through **www.plumbers.org.uk**

www.corgi-gas.com

CORGI (The Council for Registered Gas Installers) is the national watchdog for gas safety in the UK. Most importantly they maintain an up-to-date register of qualified gas installation businesses.

The Find an Installer is simple to use. Enter your postcode and select the category of service that you want and a local list of CORGI installers is produced.

www.eca.co.uk

This is the website for the Electrical Contractors Association. The association was formed in 1901 and member firms range from local employers with only a few employees, to national multi-service companies.

Although there is no legal requirement for the qualification of individuals or companies undertaking work, the pre-qualification of potential members required by the ECA means consumers need not be concerned when using an ECA member.

The Homepage has a member search tab. The search process allows you to search through a number of different parameters. But for simplicity, merely by inserting town, county or postcode, and the service you require, you will obtain a local list.

This is another professional site, and one to use in the never-ending battle against the cowboy.

SECURITY

www.nacoss.org

The National Approved Council for Security Systems recognises, inspects and regulates firms who install, maintain and monitor electronic security systems. Within the site there are links to other organisations involved in aspects of security.

The search function is comprehensive. Searches can be conducted by alphabetical index, geographical index (linked to police areas) or by simple post-code. There are many constructive options that are easy to follow, and the consumer can be confident that a professional organisation involved in security is running an extremely effective website.

HOW TO BUY THE ESSENTIAL SERVICES

www.buy.co.uk

This is a utilities price comparison service set up in 1998. The aim is to help consumers find the cheapest energy suppliers in a deregulated market.

For the homeowner the site will search energy suppliers and digital TV. It will also give some advice on water meters.

The site is extremely well laid out, and it helps if you have your current fuel bills available. It seems quite clear that there are savings to be made and this site is certainly worth a visit.

www.ukpower.com

UK Power has created a number of calculators to help consumers save money on gas and electricity. Comparisons are shown between all suppliers. The service offered is free of charge. Payment and supply is handled directly with the new supplier, although they do encourage you to switch to the new supplier through the links on the site.

This is another excellent site working in the best interests of the consumer. The comparison tables are very easy to use and all suppliers' figures are shown. Therefore you have the whole market in front of you.

It is certainly worth a visit before deciding which supplier to use.

www.servista.com

Servista was formed in 1999 and claims to be the first fully Internet based one-stop provider of gas, electricity and telecommunications for the home. Additionally they offer the consumer a single bill and bill analysis tools. In summary, the services can be managed completely through the website. The price savings are very easy to calculate. Additionally the site has an excellent question and answer section. It explains in detail how the system works. The consumer can sign up on the net.

For products you do not need to see or touch before you buy them, this sort of site has to be the future. It is certainly worth a visit.

www.thegoodwebguide.co.uk 105

ARCHITECTS

www.architecture.com

This is the site of the Royal Institute of British Architects. The site is very comprehensive. Find an Architect presents a list of both practices and individual members. For those who require serious improvements to their new home, this must be the site to use.

IF EVERYTHING ELSE FAILS!

www.yell.co.uk

Yell was launched in 1996 as an online business and consumer site providing directory services, business information and shopping facilities via the Internet. It contains a comprehensive listing of businesses – over 1.7 million in the UK – to make locating a product or service supplier easy. And since October 2000 it has included the listings in the Yellow Pages.

The search facility could not be easier. Simply enter what you are looking for, or the company, and add the location. The list provided also has location maps. If all else fails in your search for the elusive tradesman or the right piece of equipment, just Yell!

www.homepro.co.uk

HomePro was set up in 1999 to provide consumers with a reliable place to find reputable businesses. To appear on their database trade professionals must allow HomePro to take the name of up to 10 referees at random from their work files. And once they have gained a listing on the service, each new job is rated by the homeowner.

The site has a number of distinct areas.

Twenty-four-hour call out is exactly that. The rates are confirmed when you call, and the site claims that the 1,900 professionals on their system handle 85% of call outs within 24 hours.

In other circumstances, Find-a-Pro offers three ways to find your tradesman. You can enter the desired trade and postcode. You can use the national help line, or you can use the WAP Directory.

Chapter 07

protect your assets

If this is one of the largest financial commitments of a normal person's lifetime, then it makes sense to protect all the assets surrounding that purchase. And this includes everything from the bricks and mortar, to the men and women who maintain the financial infrastructure.

But insurance is not a subject we willingly embrace, particularly when there are many other costs to be met. Yet it would be madness to enter into this huge financial commitment without protecting the vital interests. This may be as important, if not more important, than the purchase itself.

It is imperative that a reasoned and responsible approach be taken to protecting your home, your possessions and your income. There is now a wide range of insurances and you can insure against virtually any liability.

And there is a clear order of priorities for protecting your assets.

General

The Government's guidance to homeowners is clear. If you have a mortgage, or are about to take one out, you should think seriously about how you would meet your mortgage repayments if you lost your income, say through unemployment or ill health. This applies equally as to how the mortgage would be paid off in the event of the death of one of the breadwinners.

The labour market is more flexible nowadays with fewer people in conventional 'full-time' employment. More people work for themselves or are on short-term contracts. Meanwhile, state support to meet mortgage repayments has been reduced. It has now become even more important for everyone to think about how they would pay their mortgage if they became too ill to work, suffered an accident or lost their job unexpectedly. The need for quality mortgage payment protection has become essential.

LIFE ASSURANCE (ESSENTIAL)

Historically mortgage lenders have always demanded that their borrowers take out life cover, so that the mortgage can be repaid in the event of their death. But in a competitive market this is sometimes left to the individual to arrange.

Life assurance is automatically built into an interest-only mortgage that is backed by an endowment policy. The policy itself provides the life cover.

A repayment mortgage or an interest-only mortgage backed by an individual savings account (ISA) or a pension will almost certainly require separate life assurance. A decreasing-term assurance alongside a repayment mortgage will pay out the outstanding sum of your loan if you die within a stated period. A joint-life policy can also be set up and the policy will pay out on the first death.

Some policies charge a slightly higher premium for level-term assurance that will pay an amount equal to your original loan.

BUILDINGS INSURANCE (ESSENTIAL)

The Buildings insurance is to cover the cost of rebuilding your home. This is not the same as the purchase price or market value of the property. It is important that the policy takes into account the effect of inflation on the cost of rebuilding. Many lenders will do this automatically within their policy renewal. And any uplift in rebuilding value must take into account any improvements to the property.

The property is the lenders security for the loan. It is obvious that lenders will not agree to a home loan without buildings insurance on freehold property. And there is a range of events that they may want it insured against, including fire, subsidence or flooding.

Lenders normally try to arrange the buildings insurance for you. If not, they will certainly make it a condition of the loan. The purpose of buildings insurance is to cover basic bricks and mortar, plus fixtures and fittings such as kitchens, baths and toilets, cupboards and interior decorations.

Policies usually cover garages and greenhouses, but often exclude boundary walls, fences, drives and paths.

It is best to shop around with this insurance. Rates are frequently based on postcode and the claims experience will vary from insurer to insurer.

CONTENTS INSURANCE (HIGHLY RECOMMENDED)

If homes are burgled, flooded or in anyway destroyed, homeowners without contents insurance will have to find the cash to replace their belongings. This can result in a disastrous financial situation. Your lender, however, will not insist on contents insurance.

Contents insurance basically covers everything that is not a fixture or fitting. The policyholder agrees a general sum assured, plus sums for individual items such as antiques, computers or jewellery. The insurance is based on either replacement as new or indemnity values. Premiums for indemnity values are lower, since the sum assured takes account of wear, tear and depreciation. Most people prefer a new-for-old policy because they get an exact replacement or even an upgraded version of the goods they have lost.

HEALTH INSURANCE (RECOMMENDED)

Heath insurance covers two areas. These are Critical Illness and Permanent Health Insurance. Critical Illness cover will pay out a lump sum if you are diagnosed as having a critical illness that is stated in the policy. This is relevant if you are concerned about losing your income in such circumstances.

Permanent Health Insurance will provide you with a monthly income should you suffer long-term sickness or disability. You can choose your deferment period. This is the period of time that expires before you start to receive income.

ACCIDENT, SICKNESS AND UNEMPLOYMENT INSURANCE [ASU] (RECOMMENDED)

Under the new Department of Social Security rules, people with a house bought after 1st October 1995 have to wait nine months before they receive help with their mortgage interest payments from the state. There are conditions and applicants must be in receipt of Income Support or Job Seeker's Allowance.

When taking out ASU insurance alongside your mortgage you can set the deferral period yourself, knowing that your mortgage payments will be covered after a certain number of weeks or months for a given period.

LAND INSURANCE (FOR CONSIDERATION)

There is now a new regulatory regime specifically for contaminated land. The legislation aims to identify sites that are polluted and to make sure that they are cleaned up.

The key principle is that the 'polluter pays' to clean up sites that are deemed by a local authority to be contaminated.

www.thegoodwebguide.co.uk 109

For the homeowner there is a particular threat. If the polluter cannot be found, the responsibility for cleaning up the site rests with the present owner or occupier of the land. The clean up will always be undertaken and there could be considerable costs involved in finding who is responsible and ensuring the land is successfully cleaned up. Also, there could be expenditure on removing the pollution. A Land Insurance policy is available through **www.homecheck.co.uk**

LEGAL INSURANCE (FOR CONSIDERATION)

For homeowners who feel they will be better protected with legal insurance to meet any legal fees, **www.find.co.uk** will provide any number of sites that offer this kind of insurance.

RESIDENTIAL LETTINGS MARKET

Landlords and tenants may need a range of protection products. The site **www.letsure.co.uk** specialises in providing insurance products and services to the lettings market.

GET YOUR PROTECTION HERE!

	Life	Buildings	Contents	ASU*	CI*	PHI*
www.find.co.uk*	x	x	x	x	x	x
www.screentrade.co.uk		x	x			
www.directline.co.uk	x	x	x			
www.swinton.co.uk		x	x			
www.lifesearch.co.uk	x				x	x
www.lifepoliciesdirect.co.uk	x			x	x	
www.a-planlife.co.uk	x			x		x
www.friendlylife.co.uk	x	x	x	x	x	

* Find.co.uk is a personal directory site with thousands of personal finance sites grouped under appropriate headings.

*ASU = Accident, Sickness and Unemployment
*CI = Critical Illness
*PHI = Permanent Health Insurance

Professional and Trade Organisations

www.abi.org.uk
The Association of British Insurers

www.adviceguide.org.uk
Citizen's Advice Bureau

www.arla.co.uk
The Association of Residential Letting Agents

www.arma.org.uk
The Association of Residential Managing Agents

www.barmovers.com
The British Association of Removers

www.biba.org.uk
The British Insurance Brokers Association

www.bsa.org.uk
The Building Societies Association

www.builders.org.uk
The National Federation of Builders

www.bwpda.co.uk
The British Wood Preserving and Damp-Proofing Association

www.cml.org.uk
The Council of Mortgage Lenders

www.dtlr.gov.uk
The Department of Transport, Local Government and the Regions

www.environment-agency.gov.uk
The Environment Agency

www.financial-ombudsman.org.uk
The Financial Ombudsman Service

www.fmb.org.uk
The Federation of Master Builders

www.hbf.co.uk
The House Builders Federation

www.iaea.co.uk
The Independent Association of Estate Agents

www.landreg.gov.uk
HM Land Registry

www.lawscot.org.uk
The Law Society of Scotland

www.lawsociety.org.uk
The Law Society

www.naea.co.uk
The National Association of Estate Agents

www.ncca.co.uk
The National Carpet Cleaners Association

www.ngrs.co.uk
The National Guild of Removers and Storers.

www.nhbc.co.uk
The National House Building Council

www.oea.co.uk
The Ombudsman for Estate Agents

www.relocationagents.com
The Association of Relocation Agents

www.rics.org.uk
The Royal Institute of Chartered Surveyors

www.rics-scotland.org.uk
The Royal Institute of Chartered Surveyors in Scotland

www.ros.gov.uk
Land Registry Scotland

www.timeshare.org.uk
The Timeshare Consumers Association

www.unbiased.co.uk
Independent Financial Advisors

Glossary for the Property Market

Absolute title. The highest and most unquestionable title to property.

Abstract of title. A summary of documents proving title.

Accountant's letter. A letter provided by an accountant to confirm income. Some lenders will accept it in place of audited accounts.

Additional Borrowing. By arranging a re-mortgage, you can borrow money against your property. This can be used for most purposes.

Additional Security. When personal borrowing exceeds a certain percentage, lenders may require additional security for the loan.

Administration fee. This is a fee charged by some lenders. It is not refundable if the mortgage does not go ahead. The fee will often form part of the valuation fee.

Advance. The mortgage loan. It is also called the capital sum or principal sum.

Adverse credit. A poor credit record such as mortgage arrears or county court judgements.

Agricultural Restriction. A freehold covenant restricting the occupancy of a property to those engaged in agriculture.

All-risks insurance. Insurance that covers all happenings that are not specifically excluded in the policy. This is different to a policy of specified risks, which covers only the happenings that are listed.

Amortisation. Period of time over which a loan is scheduled to be repaid in full by a regular series of repayments.

Amortisation schedule. This gives the breakdown of interest payments, any capital reduction and the balance outstanding at any given point during the scheduled repayment of the loan.

Annual Equivalent Rate (AER). The rate of interest that shows what the gross rate is if paid and compounded annually.

Annual percentage rate (APR). This is used to provide consumers with the true annual cost of a loan, expressed as a percentage. By law, the APR has to be shown by banks and building societies alongside their quoted rates for each mortgage. It incorporates all ongoing costs, interest charges and arrangement fees.

Appointed representative. This is a salesperson that advises on the investment products of one single life assurance company.

Apportionment. The division of liability for property tax, water charges etc. between the buyer and seller of a property.

Arrangement fee. A fee you pay to the lender in return for a particular mortgage deal.

Arrears. When you have failed to meet your regular mortgage payments you fall into arrears.

Assignment. This is the transfer of ownership to another person of some kind of property, such as an insurance policy in the case of an endowment mortgage, or a lease.

Assumption. When the seller's outstanding mortgage is passed over to the buyer of the property.

ASU (Accident, Sickness and Unemployment). It provides a monthly payment if you cannot work for an extended period due to accident, sickness or unemployment.

Attested. Witnessed.

Auction. The public sale of property to the highest bidder. At the end of the bidding the purchaser must sign a binding contract.

Bailiff. The official who repossesses your possessions or house if you cannot maintain your mortgage payments.

Balance outstanding. The amount of a loan owed at any one time

Bankruptcy. When you are either unable or unwilling to pay your debts, legal proceedings can be taken which will make you bankrupt. A bankrupt is not allowed to borrow money.

Bankers Draft. A cheque drawn on the bank itself. These are normally required in property transactions.

Base rate. The floor rate on which banks calculate interest rates. Borrowers pay a premium over base rate. Movements in the base rate are triggered by changes in the rate at which the Bank of England lends to the discount houses.

Base Rate Tracker Mortgage. The interest rate of a mortgage that tracks movements in the base rate.

Basic Variable Mortgage Rate. A lender's standard rate of interest, which is variable because it can go up or down according to economic conditions.

Bay-fronted. A property where the windows protrude from the front wall of the house.

Beneficial owner. A person owning land for their own benefit.

Benefit period. A period of time over which the interest rate of a loan is discounted, fixed or capped.

Blight. Any atmospheric or invisible environmental influence that will damage property values.

Borrow Back. If overpayments have been made, money can be borrowed back without penalty.

thegoodwebguide **115**

Box bay. A bay window built in an oblong shape with two 90-degree corners.

Bridging Loan. A loan to bridge the gap between the time when a purchaser must pay the purchase price of one house and the time when the proceeds of a sale from another house, or mortgage funds, become available.

Broker. An intermediary who will give advice and offer a range of mortgages.

Buildings Insurance. This covers the cost of rebuilding or repairing the structure of the property. Lenders insist you have enough buildings insurance before they give you a mortgage.

Buildings and Contents insurance. This is combined insurance that may be cheaper than one policy for buildings insurance and another policy for contents insurance.

Building regulations. The health and safety requirements that any new construction must meet.

Buying off-plan. This occurs when purchasers buy property from architectural plans before building commences.

Buy to Let. A mortgage designed for people who buy a property with the intention of letting it out. It is similar to other mortgages, but the maximum loan-to-value (LTV) is usually lower. Other restrictions may also apply, such as minimum letting terms and rental income.

Cap and collar mortgage. Both the maximum rate (cap) and the minimum rate (collar) payable on the mortgage are fixed.

Capital. The mortgage loan (advance or principal).

Capital and Interest Mortgage. Your monthly payments are partly to pay the interest on the amount you borrowed, and partly to repay the outstanding capital. Also known as a Repayment Mortgage.

Capital raising. This normally refers to a re-mortgage when additional funds are taken over and above the existing mortgage debt. The funds are normally used for personal finance purposes.

Capped Rate Mortgage. A mortgage repayment scheme in which there is a fixed upper limit, or cap, to the interest rate payable but where the standard variable interest rate applies when it is lower than the capped rate.

Cash Back. A cash refund incentive offered by mortgage lenders to attract new borrowers, calculated as a small percentage of the mortgage advance.

CAT-marks. This stands for charges, access and terms. CAT-marked mortgages must comply with benchmarks laid down by the Government. The Government stresses that a CAT-mark does not mean a mortgage deal is officially endorsed, and for many people non-CAT-marked deals will be a better option.

Centralised Lender. A mortgage lender who does not rely on a branch network for distribution. Centralised lending operations take their business from intermediaries or through the Internet.

Chalet bungalow. A bungalow with some first floor rooms built under the slope of the roof.

CHAPS Payment. This is a telegraphic transfer of money, normally from your lender to your solicitor. It will arrive the day it is sent.

Charge. The legal right a lender has over a property used as security until the borrowed amount has been repaid in full.

Charge Certificate. The certificate issued by HM Land Registry to the mortgagee of a property with registered title. It contains details of restrictions, mortgages and other interests.

Charges Register. One of the three registers maintained by the Land Registry for a property. It records interests adverse to the owner.

Chattels. These are moveable items such as furniture or personal possessions.

Clear title. The ownership of the property is clear and there are no legal complications.

Collar. Used in conjunction with capped interest rates. It prevents the interest rate falling below a set interest rate. This prevents the borrower from enjoying lower rates should they fall below the collared rate.

Collateral. In most mortgage transactions the property is collateral on the mortgage, and failure to meet payments means the property can be repossessed.

Common Parts. Any part of a property shared with others. It is imperative to know your rights over the common parts.

Completion date. The finalisation of a transaction. The day when the money is paid, the deeds are handed over, the keys are released and you can move into the house.

Commission. A payment made to advisors, brokers and intermediaries for selling or providing goods and services.

Conditional Insurance. This refers to insurance products that some lenders will impose as a condition of their mortgage offer. The lender could insist that that ASU or combined buildings and contents insurance is taken.

Conditions of sale. The detailed standard terms which govern the rights and duties of the buyer and the seller of a house as laid down in the contract which they sign.

Conservation areas. No building development, or demolition of property, is allowed within a conservation area.

Contents insurance. This is insurance cover against accidental damage or theft of all moveable contents, including furniture, appliances and soft furnishings.

Contract. A document that describes the agreement under which the property will change hands.

thegoodwebguide 117

Contract Race. When two or more potential buyers race to get to exchange of contracts to secure the purchase of a property.

Conveyancer. A qualified individual such as a solicitor or licensed conveyancer who deals with the legal aspects of buying or selling of property.

Conveyancing. The legal and administrative processes involved in the transferring the ownership of land, or of freehold and leasehold property, from one owner to another.

County Court Judgement (CCJ). A judgement reached in the County Court that can be for not paying debts. Many lenders will not advance a mortgage if you have any outstanding judgements.

Covenant. A promise in a deed to undertake (a positive covenant), or to abstain (a restrictive covenant), from doing specified things. They are usually contained in the title deeds. The buyer must comply with them, and they usually apply to all future owners of the property.

Council Tax. Levied by local councils to cover the cost of local amenities and services.

Credit reference. Information gathered by credit reference agencies about an individual's financial standing. They are used by organisations to assess a risk profile.

Credit scoring. A lender's way of assessing whether you are a good risk for mortgage purposes.

Credit search. A check the lender makes with a specialist company to find out whether you have any CCJs, or a record of not paying loans, credit-card bills and so on.

Critical Illness. Insurance that generally pays out a lump sum if you are diagnosed with a life-threatening illness or disease.

Current account. An account which generally has a cheque book and other facilities that an ordinary account may not have. This type of account generally pays a lower rate of interest than a savings account.

Debit card. A card that can be used to purchase goods and services. The cost of is debited directly from available funds in your account. No credit facility is available on a debit card.

Debt consolidation. The process of replacing a number of existing loans with only one loan from a new lender.

Decreasing term assurance. This is life assurance that pays out an amount if you die during the fixed term of the policy. The amount of cover reduces each year. It is ideal to cover repayment mortgages where the amount you owe the lender reduces each year.

Deeds. Legal documents assigning ownership of property or land.

Deposit. The amount of money you put towards buying a property.

Deposit account. This type of account generally pays a higher rate or interest than a current account, but there may be restrictions on access to funds. They do not generally have a cheque book or other facilities that a current account provides.

Differentials. When a lender operates a 'banding system' under which extra interest is charged on larger loans; the 'bands' are known as differentials.

Direct lender. A lender that arranges mortgages over the phone, through the post, or over the Internet.

Disbursements. Additional costs incurred such as rates, taxes, and government fees for searches, which are incurred by the conveyancer on behalf of the owner.

Discharge. When a mortgage has been paid in full and the charge is removed from a property.

Discount Mortgage. A discount offered by mortgage lenders to new borrowers, reducing monthly mortgage costs often for the first two or three years of the loan period. Once the specified period ends the discounted rate usually reverts to the prevailing variable interest rate

Dormer window. A window that protrudes from a pitched roof allowing the glass to be held in a vertical position.

Dry Rot. This is caused by a fungus and occurs when an open, potentially damp area is insufficiently ventilated.

Early redemption. Paying off a loan before the end of the mortgage term.

Early redemption charge. A fee charged by the lender if you pay off all or part of your mortgage before an agreed date, or if you move the loan to another lender.

Easement. The legal right of a property owner to use the facilities of another's land. For example, for a right of way, water, or drains etc.

Electoral Roll. This is the official voting list kept by Local Authorities. It is often used by Lenders as proof that you have lived at a particular address.

Endowment mortgage. Loan repayments combined with monthly premiums paid into an endowment policy savings plan that includes life insurance.

Endowment policy. An investment, including adequate life assurance, that can be linked to a mortgage loan to pay off the capital at the end of the term.

Engrossment. The top or final copy of a legal document. It is the actual deed for signing, and is prepared from the approved draft document.

Equity. For a homeowner, this is the difference between what the property is valued at and the amount of any loans secured against it.

Equity release. The taking of a new, larger mortgage or

thegoodwebguide **119**

increasing an existing mortgage, for home improvements, holidays etc.

Estate agency fees. The amount the estate agent charges the person selling the property. It is usually worked out as a percentage of the sale price.

Escrow. A deed delivered conditionally. It does not become effective until the condition is satisfied e.g. the other party signs his part.

Exchange of contracts. The point at which both buying and selling parties sign their copies of the contract. They are then exchanged by the respective solicitors. The agreement to buy and sell is then binding. The buyer usually pays a deposit at this point and the completion date is agreed.

Existing Liabilities. Lenders will frequently ask you to define all financial commitments, known as existing liabilities, before deciding how much they are prepared to lend.

Euro mortgages. Some lenders will offer mortgages that are paid in Euros. There is a currency risk if the rate moves against you. You could end up owing more than you borrowed. They are best for people who are paid in Euros.

Execute. To sign.

Execution only. The company selling or arranging an investment product does not give any advice on the benefit of the plan or scheme.

Failed valuation survey. When the lender turns down a mortgage application after reading the surveyor's valuation report.

Feuhold. This term is used in Scotland and applies if you own both the property and the land it stands on.

Financial Planning Certificate (FPC). This is a professional qualification for financial advisors.

First Time Buyers. The definition of this varies amongst lenders. Some lenders will define this as someone who does not have a property to sell (but may have owned before), joint borrowers where only one has owned before, or someone who has never owned a property before.

Fixed rate. This is where the interest rate is set at an agreed level over a specified term of months or years. During the specified term, regardless of whether interest rates rise or fall, a fixed interest rate will remain static.

Fixtures. Any item that is attached to a property and thus legally part of the property.

Fixtures and fittings. All non-structural items included in the purchase of a property.

Flexible Mortgage. A mortgage arrangement with flexible terms permitting payment holidays, lump sum payments at any time and variations in regular payments. Interest is calculated on the outstanding daily balance.

Flying Freehold. That part of a freehold property that is built above land that is not part of the property freehold. An example is a room built over a common access passageway.

Freehold. Absolute ownership as opposed to leasehold. The property is held absolutely for ever. Ownership is of both the property and the land it stand on.

Freeholder. Someone who holds the freehold of a property.

Full structural survey. A full structural survey looks at all the main features of the property, including walls, roof, foundations, plumbing, joinery, electrical wiring, drains and garden.

Further advance. The lender will grant you additional monies on top of your mortgage for specific purposes such as home improvements.

Gable end. The triangular-shaped vertical portion of wall at the end of the roof.

Gazumping. The person selling the property accepts an offer from a potential buyer, and then accepts a new higher offer from another buyer before exchange of contracts.

Gazundering. This is when the person selling the property accepts an offer, and then the buyer puts in a new, lower offer just before exchange of contracts.

Ground rent. An annual fee that a leaseholder has to pay the freeholder.

Guarantor. Someone who agrees to guarantee your loan and is fully liable for its repayment if you default.

HM Land Registry. The official organisation that keeps records of properties in England and Wales. Transfer of ownership has to be registered with the Land Registry.

Home Buyers report. This is an intermediate level survey that is usually offered by the mortgage lender. The report comments on the structural condition of most parts of the property that can be readily accessible, but it does not involve in-depth investigation of the testing of water, drainage or heating systems. The report should pick up most potential problems.

Home contents insurance. A policy insuring household contents against theft and damage.

Home envirosearch. A report on detailed flood, subsidence, land contamination history, and other environmental issues.

Housing Association. A non-profit making body that lets you buy a percentage share of a property, and pay rent on the remainder.

Income multiples or multipliers. A lender will work out the size of a mortgage you can borrow by multiplying your annual income by a set figure. For one person the figure is often 3 or 3.5 times income. If a mortgage is taken out jointly with a second person, their income may be added to the first multiplier. Or it may be two-and-a-half times the two incomes added together.

thegoodwebguide **121**

Income protection insurance. This covers accident, sickness and unemployment. It provides for a monthly payment if you cannot work for an extended period due to an accident or sickness.

Income references. This is confirmation from your employer that you earn the amount you are claiming in your mortgage application.

Indemnity covenant. A clause in the transfer document in which the buyer undertakes to indemnify the seller in respect of breaches in any of the restrictions in the title deeds that affect the property.

Independent Financial Advisors (IFAs). These advisors can give you information on and recommend investment products from the whole range of companies.

Interest-only Mortgage. A mortgage arrangement where the sum borrowed need not be repaid until the end of the mortgage term. Only interest is paid in the interim. The loan is often repaid by the proceeds of an investment plan like an endowment policy or a pension plan.

Insurance premium tax. This is a tax on all UK general insurance. It is currently charged at 4% of the premium.

Joint and Several. This refers to two or more parties who render themselves liable to a joint action against all, as well as to a separate action against each, in cases where an agreement is not kept.

Joint Mortgage. A mortgage where there is more than one individual named on the contract.

Joint Sole Agency. Two agents take your property onto their books and they agree to split the commission between themselves, whoever actually arranges the sale.

Joint Tenants. Two or more people holding property as co-owners. When one dies, his or her share of the property automatically passes to the survivor or survivors.

Land Certificate. The certificate issued by the Land Registry to confirm ownership of a house.

Land Registration Fee. A fee paid to verify legal title and rights over the property and to register ownership of the property with the Land Registry.

Leasehold. This is when you own the property for a set number of years. Ownership of the property is for a fixed number of years granted by lease. This does not apply to the land it is built on.

Legal charge. This is the same as a mortgage.

Lender's Completion. This is the day funds are released by your lender to your solicitor. Interest is charged from this day. This may make your first months payment higher than normal.

Legal Completion. This is the day the property becomes yours. For most transactions Legal Completion and Lender's Completion are on the same day.

Lessee. A person who takes a lease (i.e. the tenant), and to whom the lease is granted.

Lessor. A person who grants a lease (i.e. the landlord).

Level term assurance. Life assurance that pays out a lump sum if you die during the term. The amount of cover stays the same throughout the term, which makes it suitable for interest-only loans where the amount you owe stays the same to the end of the mortgage period.

Licensed conveyancer. People who specialise in the legal side of buying and selling property and who are an alternative to solicitors.

Lien. The legal right of one person to hold the property of another as security for a debt.

Link detached. A detached house with an attached garage that is itself attached to another adjoining building.

Listed Building. A building must be at least 10 years old before it can be listed for architectural or historical reasons. Consent is required for any changes.

Loan to Value (LTV). This is the size of the mortgage as a percentage of the value of the property.

Local search certificate. An application made to the local authority for a certificate providing certain information about a property and the surrounding area.

Lock-out agreement. The buyer has the opportunity to carry out essential checks and to secure funding, within a set period, without the threat of someone else purchasing the property.

London Inter Bank Offer Rate (LIBOR). The rate of interest at which banks lend their money to each other for maintaining their short-term liquidity.

Maintenance charge. The cost of repairing external and internal common parts of a building.

Maisonette. A flat with its own front door that has access direct to the outside, as opposed to access via a communal hallway.

Mortgage. A loan, usually for house purchase, and for which the house is the security or collateral. It gives to the lender certain rights in the property, including the power to sell if the mortgage payments are not made.

Mortgagee. The borrower.

Mortgagor. The lender.

Mortgage Deed. The document enshrining the conditions of a loan secured on a property. It is also called the legal charge.

Mortgage Indemnity Guarantee. Compulsory insurance required by a lender for a loan that is above the percentage of the valuation of the property at which the society will normally lend. It is also called a high lending fee.

thegoodwebguide **123**

Mortgage Payment Protection. This is insurance designed to meet your monthly mortgage payment for a limited period, usually a year, if you are unable to work through illness, disability or redundancy

Mortgage Protection Policy. A life insurance policy taken out by the borrower that will pay off the outstanding mortgage loan on the death of the borrower. It is usually taken out with a repayment mortgage.

Mortgage Term. The period of time over which the mortgage loan is to be repaid. It is commonly 25 years.

Multiple Agency. Several agents market the property, but the one making the sale obtains the commission.

Negative equity. When the total amount of loans secured on a property exceeds the property's value. You owe more money than the property is worth.

Net Income. This is the amount you are paid after income tax has been deducted.

New for old. This is insurance cover that will pay the full cost of replacing damaged or lost property with a similar, new item.

Non-status. For a non-status loan the lender does not need employment or income references from you. This type of loan is often offered to self-employed people.

Offer of Mortgage. The document issued by a lender to a prospective borrower following approval of the mortgage application. A mortgage offer is not irrevocable if circumstances change.

Offset Mortgage. Your mortgage is linked to your current account, savings accounts, other loans and, in some cases, your credit cards. The interest on your debts is calculated on the total you owe.

Open plan. A house with no internal walls to separate the living and dining rooms, and the kitchen.

Overhang. A lock-in period after a fixed, capped or discount mortgage offer has finished.

Overpayments. Irregular payments, monthly or by a lump sum, made when you can afford to do so.

Panel. Most lenders use a set number of solicitors, surveyors and valuers. This is the 'panel'. Normally you must use a professional on this list.

Pay rate. The rate of interest you pay on a home loan.

Payment Holidays. No payments are made in a month that suits you.

Percentage advance. The size of the mortgage worked out as a percentage of the price you are paying for the property.

Permanent Health Insurance (PHI). If you cannot work

because of illness or an accident, this pays a regular monthly amount until you retire, or return to work.

Permitted Development Rights. The things you can do to a property without planning permission. For example, extensions are allowed up to 15% of the size of the property

Planning permission. This is the permission granted by the local planning authority, usually the local council, for any new building, engineering operations or change of use of a building.

Portable mortgage. You can transfer your mortgage to a new home without penalty.

Preliminary enquiries. The questions asked before exchange of contracts

Principal. The amount of money that has been borrowed and on which interest is calculated.

Private Treaty. The property will change hands without appearing in an estates agent's window, or in an advertisement, or by being sold at an auction.

Property Register. One of the three parts of a Land or Charge Certificate. It describes the property and the rights that go with it.

Public Liability Insurance. This covers injury or death to anyone on or around your property.

Rack Rent. A rent representing the full letting value of a property.

Rebuilding cost. This is the recommended amount from your property valuation for which you should take out buildings insurance cover.

Redemption. The final payment of the loan, being principal, interest and costs of the mortgage.

Redemption penalties. The financial penalties incurred when repaying a mortgage earlier than an agreed date.

Regional lenders. These are mainly smaller building societies that restrict their lending to within certain regional locations.

Registered Land. This is land whose title is registered at the HM Land Registry and is guaranteed by them.

Registered Title. Title or ownership of property that has been registered at HM Land Registry.

Remaining Term. The time that is left to run on your mortgage.

Remittance fee. This is a charge made by the lender for sending the mortgage funds to your solicitor when the purchase is just about to be completed.

Re-mortgaging. Arranging a new mortgage on your home without moving.

Repayment Mortgage. A mortgage where some of the original loan is paid back with each interest payment. The outstanding balance reduces to zero over the full mortgage term.

Repossession. A lender exercises its power of sale and repossesses the property if the borrower has fallen behind significantly in mortgage repayments.

Restrictive Covenants. These are obligations imposed in the deeds on the owner of freehold property.

Retention. The withholding of part of a mortgage loan should work need to be carried out on the property in question The amount is normally the sum required to carry out the repairs, and it will be withheld until the work has been completed satisfactorily.

Rights. This is an interest protected by law as opposed to mere permission or licence, which can always be terminated. With house purchase it often amounts to a right for the benefit of one property over another (an easement). There are many types of rights, such as right of light, air, way and drainage.

Savings account. An account that pays higher interest than a current account, but may not have a cheque book. There may be restrictions on access to funds.

Sealing fee. A charge made by lenders when you repay the mortgage.

Sealed bids. When the seller asks all interested parties to place their final offer in a sealed envelope to be delivered to the estate agent or solicitor by a specific date.

Searches. Checks carried out during the conveyancing. These checks are made with local authorities and other official organisations to check planning proposals and other matters that may affect the value of the property.

Second Mortgage. This describes a loan secured on a property whose legal charge ranks second to the first mortgage.

Self-build. Where you build your own home.

Self-certification. You confirm how much you earn, and the lender does not need any references. He makes fewer checks than normal on the accuracy of the statement.

Service Charges. Fees levied on tenants by managing agents to maintain the fabric of the building.

Shared access. Part of your driveway will be shared between two or more properties. It may apply when flat-dwellers share a hallway or stairs.

Sitting Tenant. This is to occupy a property as a Tenant, and to have legal rights but without a lease. A sale would be subject to any rights of a tenant who has occupation. Such a tenant can apply to the local authority to set a fair rent. Properties with sitting tenants are generally worth 30-40% less than their open market value with vacant possession.

Sole Agency. One estate agent has exclusive selling rights for a given period, and will normally charge a lower fee.

Solicitors Undertaking. A personal guarantee given by a solicitor that something will be done.

Stakeholder. One who holds a deposit as an intermediary between the buyer and seller, so that the deposit may only be passed on to the seller with the permission of the buyer, or returned to the buyer with the permission of the seller.

Stamp Duty. A government tax payable on the transfer of ownership of a property with a purchase price above £60,000.

Standard Variable Rate Mortgage. This is a mortgage arrangement where the interest rate is varied by the lender according to conditions in the money market.

Stone cladding. A thin layer of stone or imitation stone that is attached to the external wall of a property.

Structural Survey. The most wide ranging of surveys. It is carried out by a professional surveyor. It is optional and is paid for by the buyer.

Stud wall. An internal wall made from a wooden frame rather than brick.

Subject to contract. These words should appear in every letter to the seller, the solicitor or agent, before contracts are exchanged. It is an accepted formula to stop a contract being created in correspondence.

Tandem garage. A double-length garage where two vehicles are parked one behind the other.

Tenants in common. Two (or more) people who together hold property in such a way that, when one dies, their share does not pass automatically to the survivor but forms part of their own property, and passes under their will or intestacy.

Tenancy agreement. A legal agreement designed to protect the rights of both you and your landlord. It should set out all the terms and conditions of the rental arrangements.

Term. The period of years over which you take the mortgage.

Terraced house. A house that is joined to adjoining buildings on both sides.

The National House Builders Certificate (NHBC). A certificate of sound building issued at the time of construction. It normally gives protection for ten years.

Tie-in period. As a condition of a special mortgage deal, you may have to agree to stay with the lender for a period of months or years after the deal has ended. If you move your mortgage elsewhere during this period, you may have to pay an early redemption charge.

Title. The right to ownership of property.

Title deeds. The documents conferring and evidencing ownership of land. They confirm who owns the freehold and leasehold property.

Title number. The unique reference number allocated to each property by the Land Registry

Total amount payable. The total cost of repaying a mortgage over the loan period, including the initial amount borrowed and the interest, is the total loan payable.

Top-up mortgage. When a lender does not offer enough funds to cover the cost of the property purchase, the borrower may choose to top up that mortgage with funds from another lender.

Town house. A three or four storey house with an integral garage occupying the ground floor. They are usually within a town itself and are normally terraced.

Tracker mortgages. The tracker mortgage normally follows movements in the base rate set by the Bank of England. The interest rate is set at a constant level above or below the base rate, rising and falling in line with any changes during the tracking period. Tracker mortgages tend to be for a fixed period; for example, 5 years.

Transfer deed. This is the Land Registry document transferring the ownership of the property from the seller to buyer.

Trustee. The person who has legal ownership of a property, but who is holding it for the benefit of the beneficiary.

Unadopted Road. A road that has not been accepted by a Local Authority as a result of not meeting certain standards.

Underpayments. A reduction in monthly payments.

Unencumbered Property. A property that is owned outright with no mortgages, loans or debts secured on it.

Under offer. A term applied to a property for which the seller has provisionally accepted the buyer's offer.

Unregistered Land. This relates to land where ownership is verified by a bundle of deeds that show the passing of title.

Vacant Possession. The previous occupants must vacate the property before you move in. This would include any tenants.

Valuation. A check of the property in order to determine its value. Lenders will carry out valuations on properties to assess whether they are suitable for a mortgage.

Variable rate. The interest rate that the lender charges that fluctuates with the market. A variable rate can rise or fall depending on market conditions.

Vendor. The seller

Index

Abbey National 94
Aberdeen Solicitors' Property Centre 41
abroad, see overseas
absolute;
  ownership 121
  title 114
abstract of title 114
Acceptances 94
accident, sickness and unemployment insurance 109, 111, 115, 117, 122, 125
Accommodation Directory, the 68
accountant's letter 114
accounts 114, 118
  see also, contractors, directors
additional;
  borrowing 114
  security 114
administration fee 114
advance 114, 116
adverse credit 114
advertising 23, 40, 58-68, 75
  see also, marketing
Advice On Line 78
advisors, see brokers
AER 114
  see also, mortgages
aerial images 30
agencies, see estate agents, government agencies
agricultural restriction 114
agriculture, see farms
Ainscombe & Ringland 47
air;
  quality 25, 71, 126
  travel, see transport and travel
alerts by e-mail to assist your property search, see e-mail
Alliance & Leicester 94
Allied Irish Bank 94
all-risks insurance 114
amenities, see local information and services
America, see United States
amortisation 114

schedule 114
ancillary services, see local information and services
animals 39
annual;
  equivalent rate 114
  percentage rate 114
  see also, mortgages
antiques 109
Antrim 42
apartments, see flats
A-planlife 111
appliances 117
appointed representative 114
apportionment 115
APR 114
  see also, mortgages
architects 106, 116
architecture 123
area, see location
Areacheck 70
ARLA, see Association of Residential Letting Agents
arrangement fees 114, 115
arrears 115
  see also, credit records
Arun Estates 47
Asserta Home 19, 29, 68
assets, see insurance
assignment 115
Association of British Insurers, the 112
Association of Relocation Agents, the 113
Association of Residential Letting Agents, the 68, 112
Association of Residential Managing Agents, the 112
Astute-mortgages 94
ASU, see accident, sickness and unemployment insurance
assumption 115
attested 115
auctions 64, 115
audited accounts 114
Australia 62

auto e-mail property updates, see e-mail
avoiding cowboys 103
awards 55

bailiff 115
balance outstanding 115
  see also, mortgages
Bamboo Avenue 37
banding systems 119
banker's draft 115
Bank of England 115, 128
Bank of Ireland 94
Bank of Scotland 94
bankruptcy 115
banks 16, 76, 77, 79, 81, 94-96, 114, 115
  see also, mortgages
BAR, see British Association of Removers
Barclays Bank 94
BarclaySquare 64
barns 40
Barnsley Building Society 94
Barratt 49
base rate 115, 128
  tracker mortgage 115
basic variable mortgage rate 115
Bath Investment Building Society 94
bay-fronted 115
BBC 15
BBC Good Homes 38
Beazer Homes 51
Beechcroft plc 55
Bellway Homes 54
benchmarks 116
beneficial owner 115
benefit period 115
benefits 74, 98, 109
Berkeley Homes 52
Bermuda 39
Beverley Building Society 94
Bewley Homes 58
bidding, see auctions
Birmingham Midshires 94

Blays 79
blight 115
Borders Solicitors' Property Centre 41
boroughs, see London
borrow back 115
borrowing, see mortgages
boundaries 109
Bovis Homes 58
box bay window 116
Bradford & Bingley 45, 80, 83, 94
branch networks, see centralised lenders
breadwinners 108
bridging loans 80, 94, 116
Bristol & West 94
Britannia Building Society 90, 94
British Association of Removers, the 99, 112
British Bankers' Association 16
British Insurance Brokers Association, the 112
British Wood Preserving and Damp-Proofing Association, the 112
broker 116, 117
  see also, insurance, mortgages
Bryant Homes 50
builders 21, 24, 25, 27, 34, 35, 38, 47-58, 62, 65, 103, 104, 112, 113, 117, 125, 127
  see also, trades professionals
building;
  regulations 116
  societies 12, 13, 76, 77, 79, 83, 90-96, 112, 114, 125
  your own house, see self-build
Building Magazine 48
buildings insurance 116, 117
  see also, insurance
Building Societies Association 112
Buildstore 41, 94
bungalow 117
burglary 109, 117
buses, see transport and travel
business and commercial 26, 36, 86, 106

thegoodwebguide **129**

Buy 105
buying;
  off-plan 116
  property direct 18, 58-67
buy-to-let mortgages 79, 80, 83, 84, 91-93, 116

calculating;
  mortgages 21, 22, 25, 32, 38, 46, 64, 79, 80, 82-88, 91-93
  property prices 12, 13, 16
Cambridge Building Society 94
Cambridgeshire 52
cap and collar mortgage 116
capital 114, 116
  and interest mortgage 116
  gains tax 8
  raising 116
  see also, mortgages
Capital Home Loans 94
capped rate mortgages 79-82, 84, 86, 115, 116, 124
car 86
  hire, see vehicle rental
Caribbean, see West Indies
carpenters, see trades professionals
carpet cleaners 113
cash;
  ISAs 86
  property purchases 102
cashback mortgages 81, 82, 84-86, 116
castles 40
CAT-marked mortgages 116
CCJs, see county court judgements
Cendent Relocation plc 26
centralised lenders 77, 89-94, 116
Century Building Society 94
CGNU 19
chains 52
chalet bungalow 117
Chancellors Estate Agents 47
Channel Islands, the 39, 74
change of use 125
CHAPS payment 117
Charcol 19, 28, 65, 80
charge 117
certificate 117, 125
charges, access and terms 116
charges register 117
chartered surveyors 102, 113
  see also, surveys

chattels 117
checklists for moving house 98
Chelsea Building Society 94
Cheltenham & Gloucester plc 94
cheques 115, 118
Chesham Building Society 94
Cheshire Building Society 94
childcare 98
Chorley & District Building Society 95
churches 40
cinemas 75
cities, see location
Citizens' Advice Bureau 112
city centre living 53, 62
Citylets 68
cleaning companies 98, 113
clear title 117
Clydesdale Bank plc 95
coaches, see transport and travel
coalmines, proximity to 25, 71
collar 116, 117
collateral 117, 123
colleges, see education
colour schemes, see home improvement, new home features
commission 117, 122, 124
common parts 117
commuters 11
companies, see business and commercial, directors
comparison of prices;
  property, see prices, trends
  utilities 105
completion date 117, 120
computers 109
conditional insurance 117
condition of properties 61
conditions of sale 117
conflicts, see disputes
Connell 33
conservation areas 117
consolidating debts 82, 86, 118
construction 102, 127
  see also, builders
consumer;
  advice and protection 97-112
  ratings 65, 103
contamination 25, 71, 109, 121
contemporary design 41
contents insurance 109, 111, 116, 117
Conti Financial Services 80

contractors 77, 86, 91, 108
contract 115, 117
  race 118
conversion rates 9, 39
conveyancer 118, 123
conveyancing 24, 32, 46, 58, 62, 64, 98, 100, 101, 118, 119, 126
Co-operative Bank, the 96
co-owners 122
CORGI, see Council for Registered Gas Installers
costs, see mortgages
Council for Registered Gas Installers, the 104
Council of Mortgage Lenders, the 15, 112
council tax 20, 24, 25, 61, 118
counties, see location
Country Life 40
country properties 39, 40, 74
Countrywide Assured 33
Countrywide Surveyors 102
county;
  councils 20, 75, 112
  see also, council tax
  court judgements 118
  see also, credit records
County Web Property Locator 37
covenant 114, 118, 126
Coventry Building Society 95
cowboys, avoidance of 103
credit;
  cards 86, 118, 124
  records 77, 80, 84-86, 89, 90, 114
  reference 118
  scoring 118
  search 118
CreditWeb 98
CredoRealty Deposit Guarantee 80
Crest Nicholson 58
crime 24, 70, 71, 75, 109, 117, 121
critical illness insurance 109, 111, 118
Cubitt & West 47
Cumberland Building Society 95
currency;
  conversion 39
  risk 120
current account 118, 124
  mortgages 81, 82
Cyprus 60

Dalton's Weekly 60

damage, see buildings insurance, contents insurance
damp 119
  proofing 112
Darlington Building Society 95
databases of property 15, 18, 24
  see also, directories
David Wilson Homes Ltd 53
death 108, 122, 124, 125, 127
  see also, probate
debit card 118
debt, see bankruptcy, credit records
  consolidation 82, 86, 118
decorating, see home improvement, new home features
decreasing-term assurance 108, 118
deeds 117-120, 122, 123, 126, 128
demographics 21, 24
demolition 117
dentists, see health
Department for Education and Skills, the 73
  see also, education
Department of Social Security, the 109
Department of Transport, Local Government & the Regions 112
deposit 118, 127
  account 119
  see also, calculating mortgages, mortgages
depreciation 109
Derbyshire 27
Derbyshire Building Society 95
deregulated services 105
derelict properties 93
designing, see home improvement
detached houses 14, 54, 56
developers, see builders
DfES, see Department for Education and Skills
differentials 119
difficulties with credit and payments, see credit records
digital TV 105
dilapidated properties 93, 117
direct;
  buying and selling of property 18, 58-67
  lender 119
  mortgages 77, 117, 119

130 thegoodwebguide

directions 70
Direct Line Financial Services 95, 111
Directloan 94
directories;
  builders and new developments 47-58
  estate agents 43, 44
  mortgage brokers 78
  properties 18-38, 58-68
  telephone listings 75, 106
directors of companies 86, 91
disbursements 119
discharge 119
discount;
  houses 115
  mortgages 79-82, 84, 86, 91, 115, 119, 124
disputes 100-102
  see also, legal services, ombudsmen
dividends 76
divorce 86, 102
DIY, see direct buying and selling of property, home improvement
Docklands 43
doctors' surgeries, see health
dormer window 119
Dorset 52
Douglas Allen Spiro 47
drains 119, 121, 126
drives 109, 126
driving directions 70
dry rot 119
Dudley Building Society 95
Dumfries & Galloway Solicitors' Property Centre 41
Dunfermline Building Society 95
dustmen, see refuse

Ealing 42
Earl Shilton Building Society 95
early redemption 119
  charge 119
  see also, redemption
earnings 13, 126
  see also, self-employment, unemployment
easement 119, 126
Easier 58
Easier2move 101
eating out, see hotels, restaurants
ecological interests 93, 109

Ecology Building Society 93, 95
economy, the;
  global 13
  UK 13, 115, 127, 128
Edinburgh Solicitors' Property Centre 42
education 24, 25, 29, 54, 56, 58, 70-73, 75, 98
Egg 95
elderly, see equity release, retirement homes
electoral roll 119
Electrical Contractors Association, the 104
electrical wiring 121
electricians 104
  see also, trades professionals
electricity, see utility providers
elevations 57
  see also, floor plans
E-loan 65, 81
e-mail property updates 23-25, 27-29, 33, 35, 37, 59, 64, 66
employment, see mortgages, specialist mortgages, unemployment
endowment mortgages and policies 108, 115, 119, 122
  see also, mortgages
energy;
  efficiency 93
  suppliers, see utility providers
  surveys 102
engineering operations 125
engrossment 119
entertainment 75
  see also, hotels, leisure, restaurants, sport
entitlements 74
environment 25, 56, 70, 71, 93, 109, 112, 115, 117, 121
Environment Agency, the 112
equestrian properties 39, 40
equity 119
  release 86, 91, 119
  see also, mortgages
Equus 40
escrow 120
Essex 43
Estate Agency News 45
estate agents 9, 14, 17, 19-47, 62-65, 87, 101, 103, 113, 122, 124, 126, 127

fees 120
estates 40
  see also, country properties, farms
Etours, see virtual tours
euro mortgages 84, 120
Europe 39, 74
Evening Standard, the 66
Exchange & Mart 60
exchange of contracts 120, 121, 125
exchanging, see holiday swaps, legal services
execute 120
execution only 120
executive family homes, see luxury homes
existing liabilities 120
expatriates 65, 94
experts, see estate agents, legal services, local information and services, mortgages, surveys, trades professionals, valuations
extensions 125
extras, see new home features
Ezi2buy Property Consultants 38

failed valuation survey 120
Fairview New Homes 58
farms 39, 40, 60
features of your new home, see new home features
Federation of Master Builders, the 104, 112
fees;
  land registration 122
  mortgage, see mortgages
  school 86
  searches 119
fences 109
ferries, see transport and travel
feuhold 120
Fife & Kinross Solicitors' Property Centre 42
Finance Link 78
Financial Ombudsman Service, the 101, 112
Financial Planning Certificate 120
financial services 18, 19, 28, 32, 37, 58, 61-65, 78, 79, 83, 86, 94-96, 99, 108, 112-120
  see also, mortgages
Financial Times, the 82

Find 78, 110, 111
Findaproperty 20, 42, 68
fire 108
First Direct 95
First National Mortgage Company 95
first time buyers 13, 21, 50, 55, 79, 80, 83, 120
First Trust Bank 95
Fish4homes 21, 68
fittings 109
fixed rate 120
  mortgages 79-84, 86, 91, 115, 124
fixtures and fittings 109, 120
flats 12, 14, 42, 48, 49, 54, 56, 123, 126
flexible mortgages 80-84, 86, 88, 91, 120
flooding 25, 71, 108, 109, 121
floor;
  plans 23, 49, 53, 54, 56, 57
  rates 115
flying freehold 121
forecasts 12-14, 16, 88, 92
former owner occupiers 13
for sale boards 66
foundations 121
FPC, see Financial Planning Certificate
France 36
FredFinds.com 65
freehold 108, 114, 118, 121, 126, 128
freelance workers 77, 86, 91
Friendlylife 111
FTyourmoney 82
fuel bills, see utility providers
full structural survey 121
Furness Building Society 95
furniture and furnishings, see contents, fixtures and fittings, home improvement, new home features
further advance 121
Future Mortgages 95

gable end 121
Gainsborough Building Society 95
garages 109, 127, 128
gardens 121
gas 104
  see also, trades professionals, utility providers

thegoodwebguide 131

gazumping 121
gazundering 121
geographical variations in the
  property market 11
geography, see restricted
geography
Glasgow Solicitors' Property Centre
  42
Gleeson Homes 58
global economy, see economy
Goingtomove 22
Goodmigrations 99
government;
  agencies 99, 112
  guidelines 108, 116
GP surgeries, see health
graphs 15, 71, 75, 84
  see also, demographics
greenhouses 109
green interests and organizations
  93
grid references 70
  see also, maps
gross rates 114
ground rent 121
Group 4 59
guarantor 121
guides to buying and selling
  property 18, 21, 38, 46
Guild of Professional Estate Agents,
  the 31

Halifax 13, 33
Halifax Mortgages Direct 95
Hampshire 40
Hamptons International 47
Hanley Economic Building Society
  95
Harpenden Building Society 95
headline interest 85
health 24, 54, 73-75, 98
  and safety 116
  insurance 109
heating systems 121
Herefordshire 47
Hertfordshire 47
Highland Solicitors' Property
  Centre 42
high lending fee 123
Hinkley & Rugby Building Society
  95
historical;
  land use 71

properties 123
HM Land Registry 15, 27, 38, 113,
  117, 121, 122, 125, 128
  Scotland 113
Hol365 23
holiday 86, 119
  homes 39, 41, 60, 64
  swaps 41, 64
Holmsdale Building Society 95
home;
  contents insurance 121
  see also, contents insurance
  improvement 19, 21, 23, 24, 41,
  51, 86, 106, 108, 119, 121
  see also, renovation
  services, see trades professionals,
  utility providers
  shopping 23, 64, 106
homebuyers' reports 25, 102, 121
HomeCheck 25, 71, 110
Home Counties, the 20, 47
  see also, South-East England
Home-envirosearch 71, 121
Home-exchange 41
Homefile 24
Homefreehome 60
Homepages 25
HomePro 106
Homesale 26
Homes-on-Line 23
Homes on View 37
Homes-UK 37
Hometrack 14
horseriding, see equestrian
hospitals, see health
hotels 70, 75
houseboats 40
House Builders Federation, the 113
Household Mortgage Corporation
  95
House Hunter, the 38
Housenet 63
house prices, see prices
HouseWeb 64
Housing Association 121
Housing Net 18
housing statistics 12-14, 16, 48, 75,
  115
HSBC 95
Humberts 40

IFAs, see Independent Financial
  Advisors

Igroup 95
I Have Moved 19, 99
Ilkeston Property Services 95
ill health 108, 109, 115, 122, 124,
  125
  see also, health
illustrations, see calculating
  mortgages, mortgages
impaired credit, see credit records
incentives, see cashback
  mortgages
income 114, 124
  multiples or multipliers 121
  protection insurance 122
  references 122
  support 109
  see also, mortgages, specialist
  mortgages
indemnities 37, 109, 123
indemnity covenant 122
Independent Association of Estate
  Agents, the 43, 87, 113
Independent Financial Advisors
  80, 113, 122
Independent Schools Information
  Service 72
Independent Schools of the British
  Isles 72
indexes;
  house prices 12-14
  see also, directories
Individual Savings Accounts 86
inflation 108
informing companies you have
  moved house 19, 98
injury 125
installation, see gas, utility
  providers
Institute of Plumbers, the 104
insurance 21, 24, 46, 58, 64, 65,
  77, 79, 80, 83, 85, 91, 98, 100, 101,
  107-112, 114-117,
  121-125
  premium tax 122
integrated banking mortgages 81,
  82
Intelligent Finance 95
interest 116, 125-128
  see also, calculating mortgages,
  mortgages, savings
interest-only mortgages 122
interior design, see home
  improvement

intermediaries, see brokers
international properties, see
  overseas properties
Internet, the, see online
intestacy 127
  see also, probate
investment 114, 120, 122
  see also, cash ISAs, financial
  services, Independent Financial
  Advisors, savings
IPIX 55
Ipswich Building Society 95
Ireland, see Northern Ireland,
  Republic of Ireland
Irish Permanent 95
ISAs, see Individual Savings
  Accounts
ISIS, see Independent Schools
  Information Service
islands 40
Isle of Man, the 74
Italy 39

jewellery 109
Job Seeker's Allowance 109
John Laing Homes 55
joinery 121
joint;
  and several 122
  mortgage 122
  sole agency 122
  tenants 122
joint-life assurance policies 108
judgements, see county court
  judgements

Kensington Mortgage Company
  89, 95
Kent 40, 47
Kent Reliance Building Society 95
keys 117
Kinleigh, Folkard & Hayward 47

Laing Homes Group 55
Lambeth Building Society 95
Lancashire 27
land;
  building plots 41
  certificate 122, 125
  insurance 109
  registration fee 122
  sold with properties 39, 40, 60,
  102, 115, 118, 120, 121

132 thegoodwebguide

see also, HM Land Registry
landfill sites 25, 71
landlords 68, 92, 100, 110, 123, 127
see also, buy-to-let mortgages, renting
Land Registry, see HM Land Registry
landslip 25, 71
Law Society, the 100, 102, 113
Scotland 113
lawyers, see legal services
leasehold 118, 121, 122, 128
leases, see renting
Leeds & Holbeck 95
Leek United 95
legal;
charge 122, 123, 126
completion 122
insurance 110
services 19, 21, 23, 24, 32, 37, 58, 61, 62, 64, 65, 71, 98, 100-102, 110, 113-128
Legal & General 22, 95
Legaladvicefree 100
leisure 54, 56, 58
see also, sport
lender's completion 122
lending, see mortgages
Lerwick.plc 94
lessee 123
lessor 123
Letsdirect 68
Letsure 24, 110
letting, see renting
letting companies know you have moved house 19, 98
Lettingweb 68
level-term life assurance 108, 123
LIBOR, see London Inter Bank Offer Rate
libraries 75
licensed conveyancer 123
lien 123
life assurance 64, 108, 111, 114, 118, 119, 124
Lifepoliciesdirect 111
Lifesearch 111
lifestyle 75, 93
life-threatening, see critical illness
light 126
Lincolnshire 27
link detached 123

liquidity 123
listed building 123
lists, see directories, indexes
loans, see mortgages, personal loans
loan to value 81, 82, 123
local;
authorities and councils 20, 75, 112, 119, 125, 126, 128
information and services 19, 21, 24, 25, 27-31, 37, 51, 54, 56, 61, 64, 65, 69-75, 98, 103, 118
search certificate 123
location 11, 13, 15, 19-40, 43-68, 70, 75, 102, 106, 125
see also, geographical, postcodes, regional
lock-in period 124
lock-out agreement 123
lofts 41
London 20, 27, 35, 38, 41, 42, 44, 47, 55, 62, 66-68
Londonhomenet 68
London Inter Bank Offer Rate 123
Londonproperties 68
Loot 61
Loughborough Building Society 95
low-impact lifestyles 93
loyalty cards 99
LTV, see loan to value
lump sum payments 120
luxury homes 54-56
see also, prestige properties

M25 66, 67
see also, London, South-East England
magazines 20, 31, 60, 88, 99
Mail on Sunday, the 15, 66
maintenance 123, 126
see also, trades professionals
maisonettes 14, 123
management of properties 45, 103, 112, 126
Manchester Building Society 95
Mansfield Building Society 95
maps 20, 21, 24-26, 29, 31, 45, 46, 48-52, 54, 56-59, 63, 70-72, 75, 106
Market Harborough Building Society 95
marketing 8, 17, 31, 58
markets;

money, see economy
property, see housing statistics, prices, regional variations, trends
marriage disputes, see disputes, divorce
Marsden Building Society 95
Martello towers 40
matrimonial disputes, see disputes, divorce
maximum rate 116
Mayfairoffice 40
McClean Homes 48, 49
measurements, see floor plans
medical information, see health
Melton Mowbray Building Society 95
Mercantile Building Society 95
metro, see transport and travel
Middlesex 47
Midlands, the 55
minimum rate 116
mobile;
homes 41
telephones 86
Mondial Property 65
MoneyeXtra 25, 84
money;
market, see economy
transfer 117
Moneynet 85, 94
Moneypointfinance 94
Moneyworld 24
Monmouthshire Building Society 95
monthly repayments, see calculating mortgages, mortgages
Moray Solicitors' Property Centre 42
mortgagee 123
Mortgage Express 95
mortgage;
deed 123
indemnity guarantee 123
payment protection 108, 123
protection policy 124
term 124
mortgages 13, 15, 16, 19, 21, 22, 25, 26, 28, 32, 35, 37, 39, 46, 58, 61-65, 76-96, 98, 101, 102, 108, 112, 114-128
see also, calculating mortgages
MortgageShop 65
mortgagor 123

Move Channel, the 18
moving;
abroad 8
house 97-111
see also, removals
Multimap 25, 31, 70
multiple agency 124
multiples 121
multipliers 121
mutual organizations 76

NAEA, see National Association of Estate Agents
National Approved Council for Security Systems, the 105
National Association of Estate Agents, the 30, 43, 113
National Carpet Cleaners' Association, the 113
National Counties Building Society 95
National Directory of Estate Agents, the 43
National Federation of Builders, the 112
National Guild of Removers and Storers, the 113
National Health Service, the 74
see also, health
National House Builders' Certificate, the 127
National House Building Council, the 113
National Property Register, the 38
National Register of Approved Removers and Storers, the 100
Nationwide Building Society 12, 91, 95
Natwest Mortgage Services 95
negative equity 124
neighbourhood, see local information and services
neighbours;
getting to know 28
disputes 100
net income 124
Net-lettings 68
new;
developments and homes 21, 24, 27, 34, 35, 47-58
see also, builders
home features 51, 53, 55
instructions 14

thegoodwebguide **133**

Newbury Building Society 96
Newcastle Building Society 96
new-for-old insurance policies 109, 124
New Homes 48
newspapers 21, 79, 82
New World 96
NHBC, see National House Builders' Certificate
NHS, see National Health Service
noise pollution 70
non-standard borrowers, see specialist mortgages
non-status 124
  see also, self-employment
North East of Scotland Solicitors' Property Centre 42
Northern Bank 96
Northern Ireland 42, 72, 74, 96
Northern Rock 96
North of England 46
Norwich & Peterborough Building Society 96
Norwich Union 46
Nottingham Building Society 96
Npower 30
Numberone4property 27

Octagon Developments Ltd 55
OEA, see Ombudsman for Estate Agents
offer of mortgage 124
Office for Standards in Education 72
Office of Supervision of Solicitors, the 102
offset mortgage 124
Ofsted, see Office for Standards in Education
older properties 12
Ombudsman for Estate Agents, the 101, 113
ombudsmen 101, 102, 112, 113
Onlineconveyancing 101
online mortgages 77, 117
online shopping, see home shopping
open plan 124
opticians, see health
options, see new home features
ordinary account 118
Ordnance Survey 70
  see also, maps

outdoor life, see country properties, farms, rural locations, sporting facilities
overhang 124
overpayments 115, 124
overseas;
  mortgages 80, 94
  properties 39, 62
owner occupiers 13
ownership, see deeds, landlords, title
Oxfordshire 47

panel 124
Paragon Mortgages 92
park homes 60
Park Row Associates plc 78
Partake 37
part-exchange 50, 53, 58
part-time work and mortgages 77
paths 109
payment;
  holidays 82, 120, 124
  protection 108
pay rate 124
penalties, see redemption
pensions 108, 122
percentage advance 124
performance tables for schools, see education
period property 40, 41
permanent health insurance 109, 111, 124
permitted development rights 125
Persimmon Homes 51
personal;
  finance 116
  loans 86, 116, 118, 124
Personal Investment Authority, the 78
personalizing your new home, see new home features
Perthshire Solicitors' Property Centre 42
pets 39
pharmacies, see health
PHI, see permanent health insurance
Pittis 47
place names, see location
planning;
  for moving house 98
  permission 71, 98, 125, 126

plans, see architects, builders
Plansearch Residential 71
Platform Home Loans 90
Plotsearch 41
plots of land 41
  see also, new developments and homes
plumbers 104
  see also, trades professionals
plumbing 121
police, see crime
policies, see insurance, life assurance
pollution 25, 70, 71, 109, 121
poor credit history, see credit records
portable mortgage 125
Portman Building Society 96
postcodes 14-16, 19, 21, 22, 24, 27, 29, 31-33, 43-46, 59, 61, 65, 67, 70-72, 74, 75, 100, 104-106, 109
power, see utility providers
predictions, see forecasts
Preferred Building Society 96
preliminary enquiries 125
press releases 12, 15
prestige properties 20, 46, 60
  see also, luxury homes
price/earnings ratios 13
prices 12-16, 25, 27, 65, 71, 75, 88, 115
Prime Location 28, 68
principal 114, 116, 125
Principality Building Society 96
private;
  sales, see direct buying and selling of property
  schools 72, 73
  treaty 125
probate 102
problems with credit and payment, see credit records
products, see mortgages
professionals, see estate agents, legal services, local information and services, mortgages, surveys, trades professionals, valuations
Progressive Building Society 96
property;
  market, see housing statistics, prices, regional variations, trends

search updates by e-mail, see e-mail
register 125
tax 115
Propertybroker 66
Propertyfinder 29, 98
Propertylive 30
Property Misdescriptions Act, the 17
Property Platform 31
Property Prices 15
Property-seeker 32
Propertyserviceslondon 68
Property World 37
protection, see consumer advice and protection, insurance, legal services, security
providers, see mortgages, utility providers
Prudential Assurance 47
Prudential Banking 96
public;
  liability insurance 125
  transport, see transport
Public Transport 74
pubs 40, 75
Pure Homes 62
Pure Property 38

QXL 64

rack rent 125
radioactivity 71
radon 25, 71
rail travel, see transport and travel
raising capital 86, 116
  see also, re-mortgaging
rates 119
  see also, mortgages
ratings, see consumers
ratios, see price/earnings ratios 13
Reallymoving 98
rebuilding 116, 125
  see also, insurance
receiving updates on your property search by e-mail, see e-mail
re-cycling 75
redemption 125, 127
  periods and penalties 80-86, 125, 127
Redrow Group 58
redundancy, see unemployment
Reeds Rains 46

134 thegoodwebguide

refuse 25, 71, 75
region, see location
regional;
  estate agents' lists 41, 42
  lenders 125
  variations in the property market 11, 15
registered;
  land 125
  title 125
  see also, title
  trades professionals 104-106
  see also, trades professionals
registering transfer of ownership of a property 121, 122
relocation of companies 26, 64, 98
remaining term 125
reminders, see checklists
remittance fee 125
re-mortgaging 78-83, 85, 86, 101, 114, 116, 125
removals 19, 21, 24-26, 30, 32, 37, 61, 64, 65, 98-100, 112, 113
renovation 41, 93
renting 18, 19, 21, 23-25, 28, 30, 31, 35-37, 39, 42-46, 60, 64, 68, 110, 112, 121, 123, 125, 126
  see also, vehicle rental
repairs 126
repayment mortgage 116, 118, 124-6
  see also, calculating mortgages, mortgages
repossession 115, 117, 126
Republic of Ireland 63, 94, 95
reserving a new home 50
residential;
  letting 68, 110
  see also, renting
  property, see housing statistics, prices and individual types of property listed
restaurants 75
restricted geography 85
restrictions 114, 117, 122
restrictive covenants 126
results of schools, see education
retake courses 72
retention 126
retirement homes 8, 48, 51, 55
revision courses 72
RIBA, see Royal Institute of British Architects

Rightmove 33, 45, 68
rights 122, 125-127
  of way 119, 126
Right-to-buy 86
risks, see insurance
ROARS, see National Register of Approved Removers and Storers
roofs 121
Royal & Sun Alliance 33
Royal Bank of Scotland 96
Royal Institute of British Architects, the 106
Royal Institute of Chartered Surveyors, the 102, 113
  Scotland 113
rubbish, see refuse
rural locations 26, 39, 40, 74
Russell, Baldwin & Bright 47
Ryland Technology Ltd 63

safety 116
  see also, security
Saffron Walden Building Society 96
Sainsbury's Bank 96
salespeople 114
savings 86, 92, 93, 118, 124
  account 126
Scarborough Building Society 96
schools 40
  see also, education
SCIS, see Scottish Council of Independent Schools
Scotland 27, 41, 53, 68, 72-74, 94-96, 113, 120
Scottish Building Society 96
Scottish Council of Independent Schools, the 73
Scottish Solicitors' Property Centre 42
Scottish Widows Building Society 96
Screentrade 64, 111
sealed bids 126
sealing fee 126
searches 119, 123, 126
  see also, mortgages, surveys
second;
  mortgages 126
  properties 86
security 17, 21, 51, 59, 60, 105, 114, 123
  see also, insurance

self-build 41, 86, 94, 126
self-certification 80, 84, 91, 126
self-employment and mortgages 77, 86, 91, 94
self-hire, see vehicle rental
selling property direct 18, 58-67
semi-detached houses 14
service charges 126
services, see builders, conveyancing, estate agents, financial services, insurance, legal services, local information, mortgages, removals, surveys, trades professionals, utility providers, valuations
Servista 105
settling-in 28
shared access 126
shareholders 76
Shepshed Building Society 96
shops 24, 54, 56, 58, 106
  see also, home shopping
short-term contracts, see contractors
sickness, see ill health
site details and plans 53, 54, 56
  see also, new developments and homes
Site Rider 18
sitting tenant 126
Skipton Building Society 96
smallholdings 39, 40, 60
small-scale enterprise 93
Smart Estates 34
Smart New Homes 47
social;
  security 109
  services 75
software;
  for estate agencies 36
  for financial advisors 86
sole agency 127
solicitors, see conveyancing, legal services
undertaking 127
South-East England 20, 42, 47, 52, 55, 66
South Pacific Mortgages Ltd 96
Spain 39
special educational needs 72
specialist mortgages 77, 89-94, 124
specifications, see floor plans, new home features

sporting facilities 40, 54, 56
Staffordshire 46
Staffordshire Building Society 96
stakeholder 127
stamp duty 127
Standard Life Bank 96
standard;
  variable interest rate 116
  variable rate mortgage 127
  see also, variable rate mortgages
starter homes, see first-time buyers
statistics, see demographics, graphs, housing statistics, trends in the property market
stone cladding 127
storage 19, 24, 37, 99, 100, 113
Stratford Railway Building Society 96
Streetmap 70
Stroud & Swindon Building Society 96
structural survey 121, 127
studio apartments 49
stud wall 127
subject to contract 127
subsidence 25, 71, 108, 121
summer schools 72
Sun Bank plc 96
suppliers of gas and electricity, see utility providers
support groups 74
surgeries, see health
Surgery Door 74
Surrey 40, 47
Surveyline 102
surveys 19, 22, 24, 25, 37, 40, 46, 62, 65, 98, 102, 113, 120, 121, 124, 127
Sussex 40
Swansea Building Society 96
swaps, see holiday swaps
sweeper mortgages, see integrated banking mortgages
Swinton 111

tables, see graphs, mortgages
tandem garage 127
taxation 8, 20, 24, 25, 61, 115, 119, 124, 127
Taylor Woodrow 50
Tayside Solicitors' Property Centre 42

thegoodwebguide 135

Taywood Homes 50
Taywood Lifestyle Homes 51
Teachers Building Society, the 96
TEAM Association, the 45
telecommunications, see utility providers
telegraphic transfer of money 117
telephone, see utility providers
television 99, 105
telling companies you have moved house 19, 98
tenancy agreement 127
tenants 100, 110, 123, 126-128
in common 127
see also, renting
term 127
see also, mortgages
terraced house 14, 127, 128
Terramedia Limited 30
theatres 75
theft 109, 117, 121
Themovechannel 98
This is London 35
Thomson Directories 75
tie-in period 127
timeshare 41, 60, 113
Timeshare Consumers' Association, the 41, 113
timing your move 11, 56, 99
see also, removals
tips, see refuse
Tipton & Cosely Building Society 96
Tiscali 39
title 114, 117, 118, 122, 125, 127, 128
deeds 128
number 128
see also, deeds
TMX, see Total Moving Experience
Tmxhome 32
top-up mortgage 128
total amount payable 128
Total Moving Experience, the 32
town house 128
towns, see location
tracker mortgages 80, 115, 128
Trade-It 60
trades professionals 18, 25, 33, 53, 58, 62, 65, 75, 103-106, 112
trading down 8
traffic 70
trams, see transport and travel
transfer;

deed 128
of money 117
of mortgage 125
of ownership 121, 122, 127, 128
transmitters 71
transport and travel 29, 54, 56, 58, 70, 74, 75, 98, 99, 112
trends in the property market 12-16, 75, 115
trustee 128
turnover 48, 54
see also, housing statistics
TV, see television

UCB Home Loans 91, 96
UK economy, see economy
UK Online 98
UK Power 105
UK Property Guide 18
UK Property Shop 44
Ulster Bank 96
unadopted road 128
under offer 128
underpayments 128
underwriting, see part exchange
unemployment 108, 109, 115, 122, 124
unencumbered property 128
United States, the 39, 60, 62
Universal Building Society 96
universities, see education
unregistered land 128
unusual;
employment or income situations, see specialist mortgages
properties 40
updates on your property search by e-mail, see e-mail
Upmystreet 24, 31, 51, 53, 70, 75, 98
utility providers 18, 19, 24, 30, 33, 58, 64, 65, 86, 98, 99, 104, 105
vacant possession 126, 128
valuations 12, 23-25, 32, 50, 58, 62, 79, 87, 92, 102, 114, 120, 123, 124, 128

values, see prices, trends
van hire, see vehicle rental
variable rate 116, 128
mortgages 79-82, 84, 127
variations, see regional variations in the property market

Vebra 36
vehicle rental 24, 64, 99
vendor 128
viewings 14, 17, 23, 29, 59
see also, virtual tours
village locations 26
Virgin One Account 96
virtual tours 49, 54-57, 59
voting 119

Wales 42, 46, 47, 53, 74, 95
walkthrough tours, see virtual tours
walls 109, 121
WAP directory 106
Ward & Partners 47
waste disposal, see refuse
water 119, 121
meters 105
watermills 40
waterside properties 20, 39, 40
wear and tear 109
weather 39
Web2Let 25
Welsh property, see Wales
Weslyan Financial Services 96
West Bromwich Building Society 96
Westbury Homes 56
West Indies, the 39
West Yorkshire 93
What Mortgage? 26
Wilcon Homes 57
wills 127
see also, probate
Wilson Bowden 53
Wilson Connolly 57
Wimbledon 43
Wimpey 48
windmills 40
witnesses 115
Wizards for mortgages 80, 82, 84, 87-89, 92
wood-preserving 112
worldwide properties, see overseas properties
Wriglesworth Company, the 15
Wyatt & Son 47
Wyatts 47

Yell 106
Yellow Brick Road Direct Mortgages 96

Yellow Pages, the 43, 106
Yorkshire Bank 96
Yorkshire Building Society 96
Your Mortgage 16, 88
Your Move 46, 51

other great titles in thegoodwebguide series:

hardback £12.99

antiques and collectables .... ISBN 1-903282-21-7
home and interiors .... ISBN 1-903282-15-2
museums and galleries .... ISBN 1-903282-14-4
world religions................... ISBN 1-903282-25-x

large paperbacks

the good web guide .... ISBN 1-903282-23-3 £6.99
food .... ISBN 1-903282-17-9 £7.99
gardening.......................... ISBN 1-903282-16-0 £7.99
parents.............................. ISBN 1-903282-19-5 £7.99
small businesses................ ISBN 1-903282-39-x £8.99
writers .... ISBN 1-903282-38-1 £8.99
book lovers .... ISBN 1-903282-42-x £8.99
genealogy.......................... ISBN 1-903282-48-9 £9.99

small paperbacks £4.99

comedy .... ISBN 1-903282-20-9
gay life............................... ISBN 1-903282-13-6
sport .... ISBN 1-903282-07-1
tv .... ISBN 1-903282-12-8
holiday travel online .... ISBN 1-903282-32-2
mind, body & spirit .... ISBN 1-903282-40-3
tracing your family history .... ISBN 1-903282-33-0